FOOTBALL FINAL

FOOTBALL FINAL

Selected Writings on Soccer

Edited by

Michael Parkinson and Willis Hall

Foreword by
HRH The Duke of Edinburgh KG. KT.

Pelham Books

First published in Great Britain by
PELHAM BOOKS LTD
52 Bedford Square
London WC1B 3EF
1975

ISBN 0 7207 0874 5

Design : John Elsegood

Set and printed in Great Britain by
Hollen Street Press Ltd at Slough
and bound by Dorstel Press at Harlow,
Essex

The authors' and illustrators'
royalties from the sale of this
book have been donated to the
Goaldiggers Trust.

Contents

Foreword by
HRH The Duke of Edinburgh KG. KT.

For the third year running, the Goaldiggers have produced a football anthology.

The purpose of the Goaldiggers is to help provide, or improve, football pitches or playgrounds where children and young people can kick a ball about in safety. The purpose of the book is two-fold: to provide a nostalgic dip into the history of soccer literature, and to provide money in order to construct playing fields and playgrounds where they are most needed for the future. The entire authors' royalties from the sale of this book have been donated, as in previous years, to the Goaldiggers Trust.

Willis Hall and Michael Parkinson, both founder members of the Goaldiggers Club, have once more put the book together. I hope it will be as big a success as its predecessors.

Introduction

Through all the changes in modern soccer—the extraordinary permutation of team formations, the transformation of players from wage slaves to *nouveau riche*, the escalation of a simple game to a multi-million pound world wide industry—one thing has remained constant; the lot of the soccer reporter. And that is as it should be. His job is to chronicle the change, not to join it.

The reporting of soccer is one of the most difficult occupations in the whole of journalism. It involves the resources of one man in a constant battle with time, the elements, the shortcomings of the British telephone system and the excessive use of alcohol as an anti-depressant drug and/or a substitute for the Muse who, more often than not, refuses to light on the soccer writer's shoulder at the required moment. Having squeezed into the majority of hell-holes which masquerade as press boxes we can't exactly blame the Muse for giving us the elbow on account of the kind of working conditions which would give a battery chicken the right to complain.

That soccer writers survive such conditions and, moreover, manage to fulfil their contractual obligations by writing sufficient words to cover a hole in the sports page is in itself a considerable achievement. That a few should be able to go one further and write an article which stands scrutiny at a later date, which, in other words, is fit to end its days in a book such as this and not be used to wrap round fish and chips, is nothing short of miraculous.

The miracle keeps on happening because this is the third selection of that kind of material. Not every piece in this book was written under the severe handicaps already described, but a good few were and they are the very essence of the soccer writer's craft.

Those who write about soccer for a living, who have witnessed the changes in the game we have already described, must often pause to think about their future. It must seem to them that the more television shows the big event—live or even the same evening—the more the scribe becomes shoved aside by the electronic journalist. They must feel at best the handmaidens of the new journalism, at worst superfluous. We take the contrary point of view. It is our belief that in spite of all the sophisticated engineering which goes into the televising of a soccer match one element is missing : passion, love, call it what you will.

A camera pointed at a man can tell you one thing, but nothing so profound as that same man observed by someone who knows his antecedents, who can place him in the context of the game's history and see him against the backdrop of the moment. When that happens and the information is written down and illuminated with the telling phrase, and when the emotion of the moment, not just the action, is burned on the reader's mind, then the journalist has achieved something quite beyond the scope of the camera. The one is a newsreel picture, the other is a moment of truth.

There are several such moments in this book, but that is not all there is. The collection embraces the entire scope of soccer writing, which is to say it takes into account all the different kinds of writers who feel moved to describe their passion for a game. Some of the articles are serious, some funny, some moving, others merely frivolous. But all of them deserve to stand as a testament to a great game.

One final thought. It is our considered view that not all the aforesaid changes in soccer have been for the good. It could indeed be argued that soccer, particularly at top level in this country, has been a considerable disappointment in recent years. On the other hand, it is our view that on the whole the reporting of soccer improves. One day it might be that writers whose work is represented in this book, and others who might find their way into future compilations, will have a game which is really worthy of their talents. Until that happens what follows will more than suffice.

The Editors

1

Football Fever (1)

John Moynihan

There are no limits to the fanaticism surrounding the very simple yet highly complicated game of Association Football. The average football fan may feel justified in feeling his passion for the game has reached the stages of a raging inferno, when, in reality, it only simmers in comparison with the real hard fraternity around the globe who are crazy about the game.

Some have been willing to end their lives for the game, like the Brazilian who shot himself after hearing on the radio that his country had lost in the 1950 World Cup Final; or the lady from Rio who tried to join the 'great majority' by attempting to drown herself when Pele retired from the 1966 World Cup. She was saved, and no doubt takes her seat again in the bowl at São Paulo to wave a scented hankie at the entrance of her 'millionaire' hero trotting out for Santos. And what of the memory of that desperate deed—does it hang on her back like an old spider, or has she simply forgotten it as a mad act induced by the game and the hero who overpowers her thoughts? Probably the latter—in Latin countries, the fluctuations of temperament spit and sizzle like fire crackers.

This is the age of football fever. The popularity of the game has no rival and it is played and watched by millions from Brazil to Russia, Iceland to Australia; it arouses a terrible sense of love–hate, a sense of foreboding and shock, a sense of wild hysteria caused by twenty-two little men and a white pill down there on the pitch. And up on the terraces, splashed by the wild floral colours of Mexico, or the sombre greys of Manchester, or the cherry reds of Budapest, are men and women preparing to scream and sulk, groan and weep. And all for the sake of a game Rudyard Kipling once ordained as only suitable for 'muddied oafs'. Here is an example of what this mania means.

When Leeds United played the second leg of their European Cup Winners Cup quarter-final tie against Rapid Bucharest in the

Rumanian capital, ninety York-shiremen and women, three couriers and three journalists travelled in their support on a separate charter flight. They spent just under twenty-four hours in Bucharest, a city which had just experienced its worst snowfall of the winter and had been saved from temporary chaos by an obedient population ordered on to the streets to clear drifts.

Such excursions to mysterious lands east of Vienna are now commonplace from an English football supporter's point of view, and any Iron Curtain city whose team draws an English side in the three European Cups can be guaranteed a visit from a band of loyalists bearing a degree of fana-ticism which can only be appre-ciated by travelling along with them, sharing their ale and jokes, and helping to put the odd one to bed, if and when necessary.

Only a tiny minority of the party who left Manchester Airport for Bucharest had been behind the Iron Curtain. A good proportion only had a vague idea of where Rumania lay on the map, or where the Black Sea was. The Comet's snout was simply sticking in the direction where their lads were going to play a football match, and that was 't'reason for going'. The average age of this group was much older than might have been expected. True, there was a little band of youths carrying banners and yellow pit helmets with Leeds painted in blue across the crown, and there was young Bill, a boilerman, had given up his

job especially to make the trip. But there were others of a much older age. Jim, over eighty, had fought in the Battle of the Somme in the infantry, been wounded, and hardly out of Yorkshire since. He had won the trip in a raffle and had been determined to go. There were several women on the plane who admitted they had taken the trip to cure certain unhappy states like sudden widowhood. And then, in com-parison, hearty with ale and the skills of their beloved Leeds, were the *twelve apostles.*

Wherever Leeds go abroad, the twelve apostles inevitably make the journey too, bearing an ex-troverted jollity befitting their positions as publicans, landlords and master window-cleaners from Bradford. They form a pros-perous clan on these trips, and even if their appreciation of foot-ball is somewhat biased by the habits of their beloved team from Elland Road, their love of such expeditions is deeply contagious, as was the case during the trip to Bucharest, when the whole planeload was convulsed with laughter at the wit of these gentle-men as they busily gnawed at their bangers and mash.

The Rumanian authorities at the airport appeared uneasy at our arrival and there was a long delay as passports were examined with deep interest. Big H, a master window-cleaner, had en-joyed several flagons of ale on the way out and now wobbled in front of the Rumanian immigra-tion officials like one of his own ladders anticipating a gentle breeze.

'We have a state of necessity here,' said the official gently.

A guide pushed forward. 'We have as you see a bad snowfall.'

'We have a state of necessity here,' said the official gloomily.

'Does that mean no ruddy football match, then?' asked Big H.

'No, you have your football match. The pitch has been well washed.'

'Washed, what do you mean, washed?'

'Sorry, I mean the snow has been scrubbed off the pitch.'

Michael, a student in mathematics, was the official guide to the party. On the bus going into the city he confessed puzzlement at the Yorkshire dialect. 'I cannot understand your Yorkshire it is like Chinese.' One of the Leeds supporters had enquired: 'Where's t'crumpet.'

'I am sorry,' said Michael. 'I do not understand you. All I ask for you to write down what country you were born in. You're British, aren't you?'

'Don't be daft,' said Big H. 'We're Yorkshire.'

Large blocks of snow were piled alongside the pavements and people were hurrying home from work in heavy boots and fur caps. A cinema was showing *Gone With The Wind*, and the rather drab street lighting was almost Victorian, with women huddling against the cold in shawls.

We dined in a large, palely lit banqueting-room where, from one shrouded corner, two violinists accompanied a buxom female soloist. A sense of lightly flushed awe hovered on the face of the Bradford window cleaner—Big H—as he munched his steak and turned one ear in the direction of her lament which rang shrilly across the room with the icy fragrance of a Carpathian mountain stream. 'Luverly,' he said. 'Sheer grace.'

The dining-room emptied with the veterans in the party going early to bed, perhaps trying unsuccessfully to climb into a deep Edwardian plunge bath with rusty silver taps which gave this Bucharest hotel a flavour of *The Prisoner of Zenda*.

'The Leeds players will be in bed by now,' said a Leeds commentator. 'There's no going out for a drink with Don Revie. They are here to play football. He tucks them up like Teddy Bears for the night just as soon as they've had their meal. Big grown-up Teddy Bears ready to be wound up the next morning and sent out on a football pitch. You wouldn't think they were human beings, would you? But they wouldn't win a thing otherwise. Revie's a good manager, but he can be difficult to get to know.'

These supporters' trips are usually divided between the hell-raisers—in this case Big H and his twelve apostles plus the youngsters—and the older members who have come, generally as raffle-prize winners, to have a bit of sightseeing and see the match. In due course, after loafing around snow-encrusted city streets, they found a night-club offering a sexy cabaret with gipsy dancers and expensive beer which was swept back in torrents. A Leeds farmer, a wealthy gentleman with a rubicund, jolly face, remembered the days when he used to send his stable straw down to the Leeds football ground, Elland Road, to lay on the pitch on frosty nights before a match. 'We used to collect the straw after the match, and it was twice as heavy —full of bottles and umbrellas and handbags.'

'Any bodies, Tom?'

'Not that I noticed—but there might have been.'

The evening ended waveringly with Big H singing a solo song of piercing gusto: '*LEEDS ARE THE GREATEST.*'

Dawn was watching a Bucharest fatigue party shovelling

"If we're going to be this close, how about ghostwriting my column in The Sun?"

snow into a lorry, a Rumanian army major watching querulously at the wavering passage of some merry Yorkshiremen. Big H appeared on the foyer of the hotel in his underpants singing 'God Save The Queen'. He was helped to bed by a hotel porter, who beseeched him to 'Lie down, pleece.'

'Why should I lie down? I want to stand up. Sing us a song, Ivan.'

The next morning, the Leeds footballers rose, feeling refreshed and rested in their elegant suites at the Inter-Continental hotel. Outside their windows, the city looked yellowish-pink in the sunlight. The snow was melting below as elderly women hunched their shoulders over brooms and pushed the melting slush into heaps. The Leeds supporters at their own hotel—the ones who had stayed up late—woke up feeling rather more bilious than Mr Revie's men. Big H observed his scrambled eggs at breakfast like a man about to be trampled by an African elephant.

The bus to the stadium left at two o'clock and Big H and party had already cheered up noticeably by then. There was a surge of reminiscence about the night before, although Big H could remember little of it. The veterans had been on a sightseeing tour of the city, and a man who had been to Bucharest before said he thought the residents were looking less sad than they had done previously. The Rumanians, the young ones, the students had enough pride in their country to give it a certain independence. The match between Bucharest and Leeds had been given three paragraphs in the local party newspapers stating the event but making no comment about the outcome. With Leeds already five goals clear, the outcome wasn't really worth considering, but the English newspapers in comparison had written columns about it.

The stadium where the Yorkshire supporters were taken was a stark, chilly bowl, the pitch swept of snow, well away from the supporters. Groups of small boys were climbing into the ground for free entrance by dropping into large snowdrifts from trees overlooking the terraces. It was not they who interested the police, but the more affluent party members who suddenly made a tiny cavalry charge on the most expensive entrance, forcing the policeman's fur cap off his head and squeezing through. The hooligans of England are generally young, but these fur-jacketed party members, scrambling to get by, behaved with a fierceness which almost overwhelmed the law. It was all over in five minutes, the breach made and evidently allowed. The Leeds supporters were shown to a block in the stand carrying their yellow favours. There was a cold chill in the air and pools of water formed on the steps. Big H and his friends bought a case of beer outside and started a party going at the top of the stadium. The arrival of the Leeds players on the pitch produced a gargantuan roar from Big H's throat.

The roar was amply rewarded after a minute's play when Eddie Gray in his canary-coloured strip moved up from midfield, drew the full-back Grigoras, and Bates sneaked through to push the ball past Raducanu. Big H was so overcome by this early goal that he failed to notice a Rumanian with little ferret eyes steal away with one of his crates of beer. But Big H wouldn't have cared— Leeds were a goal up and he and the other apostles slapped each other on the back until the ball had been kicked off again, kicked into the Leeds penalty area, and Madeley had promptly handled the ball to give away a penalty.

The whole stadium was hushed as a local hero called Neagu prepared to take the kick. Army officers and NCOs among the spectators came visibly to attention as Neagu snapped back his shoulder-blades, eyed the Leeds goalkeeper, Harvey, as if he was about to run through him, and then set off on his run. He ran and ran and at last connected with the ball and the twelve apostles were all looking the other way because they hated seeing their side concede a goal. But Neagu hit the ball wide of an upright into a snowdrift and held his head in mortification as his fans groaned and whistled. 'I feel really sorry for him,' said Big H. 'The lad really thought he'd got one.'

With Leeds 6-0 ahead on aggregate, the match became an academic exercise for them. They kept possession, avoided the most scathing of the Rapid tackles, and moved on comfortably to win by 3-1, Jones scoring a goal in each half. The most entertaining feature of the match was the goalkeeping of that eccentric giant, Raducanu, whose arms seemed to stretch down to his ankles. Lorimer was astounded once by Raducanu's slide tackle after he had dribbled past the goalkeeper and was about to tap the ball into the empty net. Such eccentricity was enjoyed by the home crowd until the goalkeeper ran out of goal like a kangaroo setting off on a long desert expedition and Jones simply bent beneath one of Raducanu's arms and scored off the top of his head.

With Leeds having won 8-1 on aggregate, their place in the semi-finals assured, there was plenty to cheer about on the coach trip to the airport. The players and officials left on the first plane, and when they strode through the airport lounge the supporters were waiting to cheer. But the players looked straight ahead, ignoring their fans as if embarrassed by the fuss. It seemed a little unkind. They might have turned their heads right and smiled at the young group of fans, or they might have turned their heads left and waved at the older fans hailing them. But they didn't; they kept walking forward and went down in the estimation of we neutrals who were watching.

Back at Manchester Airport a few hours later, the fan party mingled with each other, saying they would meet again in Greece in the final.

'Now I'm off to milk the cows,' said the farmer.

'You've got to be someone who can adapt to others' company,' said Big H, clutching his duty-free goods. 'It's no use being long-faced.'

From *Football Fever*, 1974

FOCUS ON FACT —*The Football Story (1)*   **By Gary Keane & Neville Randall**

SATURDAY, AUGUST 17. THREE-QUARTERS OF A MILLION SPECTATORS RETURN TO THE FOOTBALL TERRACES. ANOTHER 20 MILLION BET FROM 4 TO 5 MILLION POUNDS ON THE RESULTS THROUGH THE POOLS.

ANOTHER ENGLISH SOCCER SEASON BEGINS.

FOOTBALL IS PLAYED BY A MILLION IN BRITAIN: 16 MILLION IN A QUARTER OF A MILLION CLUBS IN 142 COUNTRIES ROUND THE WORLD. AND BY NEARLY EVERY SCHOOLBOY EVERYWHERE.

IT IS WATCHED — ON WORLD CUP FINAL DAY— BY 1,000 MILLION ON TELEVISION. AROUSES ECSTASY, ANGUISH, ARGUMENTS AND VIOLENCE. AN OPIATE, RELIGION, OR JUST THE MOST POPULAR GAME IN THE WORLD?

2

Football Grounds of the Riviera

Alan Ross

Rock-cut, railway flanked, with sea edging its flat
Surface, Monaco hangs top-heavy over dwarfed white posts:
Casinos and aquariums bulge above the crenellated coast,
Arc lights strung along the stadium, like cloche hats.
Below, the pitch is smooth as green Casino baize
Whose wheels spin over water pink with haze.
Coated in sunset, the harbour's neat, dark palms,
Like roulette players, keep stiff their salt-drenched arms.

Scrambling over bald, dusty, but flower-scented ground,
Cactus gesticulating, olive-edged, make-shift, and public-owned,
Ventimiglia's forwards fan out round Bordighera's goal,
Jerseys striped like fishes in a noisy shoal.
Mountains bisect the sky with rocky signature
And sea-air modifies the players' temperature.

Mauve waves grow taut and spray the piazza pines,
As fishing boats trail their lamps in golden lines.

Menton at home to Nice, the French League leaders,
Sun only a rind squeezed dry of its heat,
And below us the voices of bathers scratch
At the cellophane air, airing ignorance of the match.
The tide recedes, drawing yachts in gentle retreat.
Outlined against mackerel sky, rack-bound readers
Golden indulgent flesh, absorbed in their books' spilled flush:
The insentient frontier hardens, the coastline in ambush.

3

A Voice in the Crowd

Alan Simpson

Dearly Beloved, the text of my sermon for today is taken from the Gospel according to Hardacre, Chapter X, Verse XXIII. 'Two's company three's a crowd.' Well, at least it is in the Spartan League. Yes, brethren, my remarks today directly concern you lot . . . the crowd. I love football crowds. There is something wonderfully British about a gathering of people, for the most part eminently respectable, who conduct themselves during the week with the utmost decorum, and then on a Saturday afternoon, quietly line up to hand over their 25p at the turnstile so they can spend the next ninety minutes screaming abuse at twenty-two players, a referee, two linesmen, two managers, and anybody else who looks as if they might have something to do with it, and then, when the final whistle goes, file quietly out of the ground, back to their homes and jobs until the next Saturday when the red mist overtakes them again. I often wondered where Robert Louis Stevenson got the idea of Dr Jekyll and Mr Hyde. Now I know.

He was at a football match.

Strangely enough the thing that a screaming angry crowd can't stand more than anything else is players shouting. This really gets up the average spectator's nose. They have only to hear a player shout out 'My ball', 'Man on', 'Turn', etc, and they go potty. Of course, in a top professional game with a crowd of over 50,000 yelling people, one cannot hear the players calling and so the crowd don't get so upset about it, but in an Amateur game, in front of around 500-1,000 people one can hear every word the players say, and the effect on the crowd is quite remarkable. There is one gentleman here at Hampton who stands on the Kop near the stand and who gets particularly irate when the players call to each other. Thus they have to shout louder, which only makes him shout louder to stop shouting, and so on. As soon as we get the *Meggezones* on sale at the sweet counter we'll make a fortune out of it. As far as I'm concerned, anybody who has paid their 25p is entitled to do what they like. Let's face it, after being shouted at by the wife all week it's nice, for such a small cost, to get your own back and shout at someone else for a change. At least we haven't had to dig a moat round the ground yet.

Another thing I love about football crowds is their attitude towards dirty play. There is, in fact, a mathematical equation which can be applied to this. It is simply that the difference between a dirty, vicious, over-the-ball piece of diabolical clogging and a beautifully timed, superbly played, scientific tackle, is in direct proportion to the colour of the shirt the player is wearing. The same equation can also be applied to offside decisions, throw ins, hand balls and thumping the referee. Although I must say that the crowds we get at Hampton are much more sophisticated than those at many grounds. This is most noticeable in the quality of the toilet rolls. Nothing but Soft Pastel Shade 'Delsey'. We don't throw any old rubbish down here.

Of course, the wit of English football crowds is legendary. And rightly so. I'd like to finish by giving you two examples, both of which are absolutely true. I know, because on both occasions I was present. The first time was at Stamford Bridge in August, 1955. If you remember, Chelsea had won the League Championship for the first time in their history. This after years of being the laughing stock of the English First Division. On the opening Saturday of the next season, their first ever as Champions, they began their programme at home to Bolton Wanderers. Twenty-five minutes before the kick-off the entire Chelsea team ran out onto the pitch carrying the Championship Shield. They did a lap of honour in front of a packed crowd who responded with the loudest prolonged cheering I have ever heard at a football ground. It was quite emotional. Strong men were seen to weep. The team ran back into the dressing-room, and then ten minutes before kick-off came out again, once more to a fantastic reception, to line up for an official team photograph with the Shield. The ground was a cauldron of excitement. It really was a moving experience. Finally, the game was ready to start. The captains tossed up, Bolton Wanderers won the toss, and Chelsea kicked off. Centre-forward Roy Bentley tapped the ball to his inside-right, and a man standing next to me bawled out, 'Oh, God blimey, same old Chelsea !'.

I hope our female supporters will forgive me for the slight vulgarity of the second instance, but I really think it's worth telling. This time the scene was Griffin Park. George Poyser had received a full-blooded volley from close range straight in the . . . well, let us say in the nether regions a little south of the lower abdomen. As he lay there pole-axed on the ground, the stadium was in complete silence. I think every red-blooded man in the ground had felt the blow. A pin drop could have been heard. And then, as the Brentford trainer reached Poyser, took out his sponge and pulled back the elastic of his shorts, a loud voice from the terrace was heard all round the ground. 'Don't wash the bleeding things—count 'em.'

Brethren, enjoy the game, and if you think our players are shouting too loud, don't be too hard on them. After all, they've been shouted at all week by their wives as well.

From the *Hampton Town F.C. Programme*

FOCUS ON FACT—*The Football Story (2)*   By Gary Keane & Neville Randall

HOW DID FOOTBALL BEGIN? GREEKS AND ROMANS PLAYED A GAME CALLED HARPASTUM. PASSING A SMALL, HARD BALL BY HAND ON A RECTANGULAR FIELD, TO GROUND IT BEHIND THE OPPONENTS' LINE. ROMAN SOLDIERS PROBABLY BROUGHT IT TO BRITAIN AND GAUL.

1066. NORMANS INVADED BRITAIN. PERHAPS BRINGING A GAME DERIVED FROM HARPASTUM, PLAYED IN BRITTANY AND NORMANDY, CALLED LA SOULE. LIKE A GAME RECORDED IN GLOUCESTER CATHEDRAL.

1195. WILLIAM FITZSTEPHEN, MONK AND FRIEND OF THOMAS 'A BECKET, DESCRIBED A LONDON TRADITION ON SHROVE TUESDAY.

"ALL THE YOUTH OF THE CITY GO TO A FLAT PATCH OF GROUND JUST OUTSIDE THE CITY FOR THE FAMOUS GAME OF BALL." FOOTBALL?

FOCUS ON FACT—*The Football Story (3)*   By Gary Keane & Neville Randall

MEDIEVAL BRITAIN. IN LONDON AND OTHER CITIES MOBS RAMPAGED THROUGH NARROW STREETS, KICKING A BLOWN-UP PIG'S BLADDER, BREAKING WINDOWS AND PLAYERS' LEGS, FILLING PEACEFUL FOLK WITH FEAR.

IN THE COUNTRY, ON PUBLIC HOLIDAYS, YOUTHS IN TEAMS OF SOMETIMES 500, ENGAGED IN DAY-LONG STRUGGLES TO FORCE A BALL ACROSS BOUNDARIES MILES APART. MOB FOOTBALL.

STILL PLAYED AT ASHBOURNE, DERBYSHIRE, ON SHROVE TUESDAY.

1388. KING RICHARD II ISSUED A PROCLAMATION.

"SERVANTS AND LABOURERS SHALL HAVE BOWS AND ARROWS AND USE THE SAME ON SUNDAYS AND HOLIDAYS, AND LEAVE ALL PLAYING AT BALL WHETHER HANDBALL OR FOOTBALL."

FOCUS ON FACT—*The Football Story (4)*   By Gary Keane & Neville Randall

17TH CENTURY. FLORENCE. GENTLEMEN PLAYED A BALL GAME CALLED CALCIO. TEAMS OF 27 DEFENDING A GOAL LINE THE LENGTH OF THE FIELD.

IN BRITAIN SIR THOMAS ELYOT WROTE: "FOOTBALL IS NOTHING BUT BEASTLY FURY AND EXTREME VIOLENCE."

PURITANS FAILED TO SUPPRESS IT. CAMBRIDGE UNDERGRADUATES PLAYED INTER-COLLEGE MATCHES. AMONG THE KEENEST "MATCH-MAKERS AND PLAYERS OF FOOTBALL" WAS A YOUTHFUL OLIVER CROMWELL.

COUNTRY FOLK PLAYED SPIRITED MATCHES ON PUBLIC HOLIDAYS. THE GAME SPREAD NORTH. CONTEMPORARY SCOTTISH HISTORIANS REPORTED "COMMON PEOPLE MUCH ADDICTED TO FOOTBALL AND GOLF."

4

European Football

Hunter Davies

We had to be at London Airport at two o'clock on the Tuesday to board a BEA charter plane for Nantes in France. As we were checking in, a TV crew were standing waiting, their lights at the ready. 'Must be waiting for Martin,' said someone and the others agreed. But when Martin appeared, the one and only Martin of the moment, the cameramen weren't at all interested.

The Spurs party consisted of thirty-five people. There were sixteen players, eight directors and officials, ten journalists and Mr Broderick of Cooks who'd arranged the trip.

It was a normal-sized party for a British football team going into Europe. The cost of the plane was about £1,500. Spurs usually hire their own plane when they play abroad as it's more convenient, letting the Press for once join the inner sanctum. But no fans are allowed on the team plane.

Mr Broderick spends his whole life organising football trips, for clubs like Spurs, Chelsea and others, plus the England team. He'd recently taken the England

party to Switzerland. He prefers going with the England team, though not for snob reasons. 'With the England team there's a nice atmosphere because it's mainly old friends meeting each other again. With a club, they see each other every day of the week.'

At Nantes airport, there were photographers and a TV crew waiting to meet the Spurs team as they climbed out of the plane. Greetings were exchanged with the Nantes officials who said there would be a reception next day, Wednesday, for the Spurs directors and the Press. Bill Nicholson thanked them but said he was more interested in visiting the stadium. It was agreed he could see it at eleven the next day.

The local Press went straight for Chivers, running after him, and shouting Mee-ster Chee-vers. They got him to pose with a toy pistol, pretending to shoot. His legend had preceded him, even to Nantes, wherever Nantes was. None of the players had the slightest idea, or were even interested.

We went by coach to the

Central Hotel in Nantes, a modest medium-sized hotel, nothing like as posh as most of the English hotels Spurs use. Bill Nicholson had chosen it personally, vetting the rooms and meals. He'd come over on a quick trip the week before, mainly to scout on the Nantes team. As usual, he'd left nothing to chance, but he'd been even more meticulous this time, as it was Europe.

Playing in Europe is both an end and a beginning for the top British clubs. It's in their minds all season knowing that if they finish high enough in the English league, they will end up qualifying for one of the three European competitions the following season.

Spurs were now in the second round of the UEFA Cup—the Union of European Football Association Cup. Each round is played on a home and away basis, with the winner on aggregate of the two matches going into the next round.

Sixty-four teams had started off from every footballing country in Europe back in September and several famous ones had already been knocked out, such as Leeds United and Atletico Madrid, though traditionally the first round is looked upon as a walkover for the big clubs. It had been for Spurs, playing the Icelandic amateurs. But now it was serious. Having a good run in Europe can keep a club going for nine months, a whole season in fact. It keeps the players on their toes, the fans happy and brings in money to the club.

They knew they would have a hard struggle with Nantes. They had twice won the French League in recent years so they'd had good experience of European football (Celtic had knocked them out of the European Cup in 1966). Although French football journalism is of a high, nay, intense level, French football is not as well supported as English. Nantes average gate is considered very good in France, eighteen thousand, only half that of Spurs.

The Spurs directors were making no bones about what a pleasure it was to be in Europe again, but many of the players were coming on strong about it being a drag. The ones who'd played in France before were telling the others there was no chance of any talent after the match. The French didn't like the English. Their girls wouldn't even dance with you, unless you paid them a fortune. Now Germany, you always had a good time in Germany.

We checked in quickly at the hotel and the players went into their own dining-room for a light tea while the Press and directors went into the main dining-room.

As they waited for their meal, the players were all comparing their rooms. 'How's your TV? Only one of mine's got colour. Got a bar? We've got a bar. Cyril's got a swimming pool in his room.' They were complaining, in their usual inverted fashion, about the hotel. They all thought it was pretty crummy with no

facilities. It wasn't luxury by any means, but very French with a kind staff and a friendly atmosphere. The players ordered toast and tea and had hysterics when the toast arrived wrapped in plastic, like babies' rusks. They tried to butter it and immediately it disintegrated into crumbs. But there was strawberry jam which they loved.

After tea most players put their heads out of the front door. It was raining and dark. Several had wanted a walk but when they saw the rain, they went back to the foyer, sat chatting or playing cards. The regular card players, Joe, Gilly, Mike and Cyril had got down to it the minute tea was over without looking at the weather.

Phil, Roger, Jimmy Neighbour and myself decided to chance it and we made a dash between showers. We got fifty yards from the hotel and took shelter in a souvenir shop. Phil picked up a pair of moccasins and indicated that he wanted a larger size. The assistant nodded and went to get bigger ones. Phil spread his arms about two feet wide and she nodded, though beginning to

25

think she'd got the order wrong, or was serving a madman. Phil put one finger up and said One, he only wanted one, then left the shop.

Roger picked up a paper knife and was pretending he was going to throw it at the wall. The lady took it from him and held it in front of her chest, defending herself, convinced they were madmen, trying to push Roger out of the shop.

Roger came out at last, laughing. 'She said Sootie, Sootie. What does that mean?'

Dinner for the players was at seven-thirty, served in the same dining-room. Bill spent at least an hour going through the menu, standing in the middle of the room and reading it out, getting them to show by a show of hands what they wanted. Not just for the meal that they were about to have, but for the next day's meals as well. It was a job Johnny Wallis could have done, or Mullery, or the head waiter, or anyone.

The choice of main course was veal or steak. At the table I was at, Phil and Roger and Jimmy had steak but left almost all of it. It arrived with a little daub of garlic butter on the top and they tore at it furiously, swearing, and wiped all marks of it from their steak. They all said they hated garlic. Phil even washed his hands on his napkin, pouring water on them from a jug, in case he'd been contaminated. I ordered beer but the players couldn't. The hotel staff had been given instructions that no player could have beer or alcohol of any kind, at the table or in his room, not till the match was over.

Bill, his orders finally completed, went to eat with the directors in the main dining-room. When he'd gone, the bread pellets started flying and then the grapes, but nothing out of hand and no clothes or tables were ruined. The waiters were amused, when they weren't pointing out to each other which one was Cheevers.

Throughout the entire meal, all four courses of it, the card school played cards non-stop, dealing on the table over the vegetable soup, trout meunière, the steak and the fruit salad, all of which was delicious, much better than any English hotel food, that's if you don't mind garlic.

As we left the dining-room, Roger saw a notice above the door which said 'Sortie' and asked what it meant. I said exit. 'That's it. Sootie. That's what she said.'

After dinner, they all sat around in the hall, the card players still hard at it. The Press decided they'd go out and see the town, plus me, and Mr Broderick, the Cooks man. We all discussed our plans loudly, about the night-clubs we were going to, knowing the players were confined to barracks.

As we went out of the front door, Eddie Baily and Johnny Wallis were standing there, four square and resolute. They were on guard to make sure that no players sneaked out with us.

Next day the morning paper,

Nantes Océan, had a picture of me on their front page, coming down the ladder from the plane. Beside me was David Miller from the *Telegraph*, Colin Malam of the *Sun*, Steve Curry of the *Express* and Nigel Clarke of the *Mirror*. The caption underneath said 'The stars of the celebrated Tottenham team arriving at Nantes airport yesterday.' That kept the team in jokes all day.

At eleven o'clock, I went with the players for a brief visit to the stadium, then they went back to the hotel to put in the time until lunch, going through their usual monastic rituals, no fun and no alcohol, simply playing cards or taking an occasional walk round the block, hour after boring hour.

Meanwhile, I went with the Press and the Spurs directors to a slap-up reception at a hotel ten kilometres out of Nantes, given by the Nantes Football Club. We had lots of wine, a three hour lunch and several speeches. The big lads from the Paris Press had now arrived, wheeled out for the match, to show the local lads how to write correct captions. They knew the names of every Spurs player. All of them seemed to be from *L'Equipe*.

Back in Nantes, I went shopping in the afternoon with a couple of directors. We went to a superb cheese shop, taken by a Nantes director. Mr Groves, the bachelor, bought six. Then he bought six bottles of Muscatel. Back at the hotel, you could tell the players from the directors. One lot had bought souvenir dolls and the other carried wine bottles and smelled very strongly of cheese.

While the Press and the directors had been enjoying themselves hugely all day, lapping up the entertainment which the players' success had brought them, the players themselves had still been hanging about the hotel. They were obviously feeling the strain of waiting. They'd just finished a one and a half hour team talk from Bill. He'd gone through every Nantes player in detail. They couldn't wait for the match. They were all fed-up and bored rigid with waiting.

We left the hotel by coach at seven fifteen. By now the hotel was full of Spurs supporters— seventy of whom had just arrived. Suddenly the foyer had become crowded with middle-aged Englishmen in their best Sunday suits and supporters club ties, wandering round wearing blue and white rosettes and ogling the players.

The streets to the stadium were crowded but the bus got through fairly easily. Along the final stretch were rows and rows of stalls selling nougat, hot dogs, sweets and drinks, ham rolls and other delicacies. Unlike a British ground before a match, nobody seemed to be selling rosettes, scarves, badges or other football souvenirs. Food and drink seemed to be the only line for all the street traders. The crowds too appeared different, older and better behaved, a lot of them wearing tartan berets. There were no gangs of young hooligans trying to assert themselves or looking for fights. But inside the stadium, they made just as much noise if not more than a British crowd. When the songs started, the whole crowd joined in. At Tottenham, it's just the Park Lane end who sing the songs. The French crowd communally sing, the way they do at Welsh Rugby Union matches.

The dressing-room, like the stadium, was spartan and seemed to be made entirely of concrete. On the benches round the dressing-room was a new bar of soap and a new blue towel for each player to use, still in their wrapping papers. Most of the players pocketed the soap in its wrapper. 'Another free present for the wife.'

Peter Collins, who was suffering from diarrhoea, was given some pills by the Spurs doctor and told not to eat anything for twenty-four hours. Then, along with the directors, the doctor discreetly withdrew, leaving the manager and the players to get on with their rituals.

A French official opened the dressing-room door and looked in and Philip Beal shouted at him. Philip beckoned with his hand, wiping his bottom and saying in English that there was no lavatory paper. Everyone laughed, thinking it was another Philip Beal joke. A few minutes later the official reappeared with a packet of paper and everyone cheered as he threw it across the room to Philip.

'Well played,' said Roger Morgan. That was his catch phrase of the moment. He'd said it to every

waiter in the hotel since we'd arrived in Nantes.

'It's good to have one joker in the team,' said Eddie Baily heavily and sarcastically. 'A joker always helps.' He was busily massaging Steve Perryman's thighs with warm oil.

'Is that why you bought Roger,' someone shouted. Everyone was looking at Roger, to see how he reacted. They were no doubt thinking of an article in the previous week's *People* in which Roger Morgan had been described as one of Bill Nicholson's expensive mistakes. Roger must have been very hurt. It hadn't been his fault that he'd been injured and not played in the first team for a year.

Roger made a face, his head bowed, pretending to be hurt and embarrassed, but laughing, putting it on, not at all worried by the joke at his expense. Roger is one player who'd be very difficult to humiliate by sarcasm. Not because he's very thick-skinned, or even conceited, but because he takes it all as a joke anyway. He'll try hard, but not playing for the first team is not the end of the world to Roger.

Underneath the table was a brown cardboard box. Bill Nicholson picked it up, put it on the table and opened it, saying there was a present inside for everyone.

'They asked me for a list of things you'd like, but I don't know which one they chose,' explained Bill. 'If it had been me, I'd have given you a comb and a pair of scissors each.'

The players ignored the joke, having heard it a hundred times before, and rushed forward to get their presents. They'd been individually wrapped in green paper and tied with a bow, just like a Christmas present. Roger was first to tear his open so they all watched, deciding to keep theirs nicely wrapped up. Another free present for the wife. Inside was a black present box containing a Waterman's propelling pencil. 'Great', said Roger. 'The box on its own will do as a present.'

'Made in Hong Kong, mine says,' said someone, pretending to read the label.

'Nantes,' said Mullery.

'Nantes-sense,' said Chivers, walking across the room to the shower, repeating his joke on the way, but still nobody got it.

An official appeared and told Bill that the teams were to come out five minutes before the kick-off. The match was to begin at eight-thirty. It was now ten past eight. The room was getting quieter. The time for jokes was over, if you could call them jokes. It had been self-conscious noise and chatter, and an outlet for their nerves.

Joe Kinnear was doing exercises on his own in a corner. Outside, inspecting the pitch, he'd been shivering. An evening chill had descended, but he was obviously nervous.

Martin Peters asked Bill if he knew the referee. Bill said he was an East German, but he'd forgotten the name, which was unlike Bill Nicholson. Martin thought he might be the same East German ref they'd had in the World Cup. Bill said he didn't think so.

None of the players had programmes. In an English dressing-room, the players are always amply supplied with free programmes. I had got one at the hotel from a French journalist. It was a simple, four-page, folded-over programme, full of adverts. Leslie Yates, a free-lance journalist who writes the Spurs programmes, had come specially to Nantes so that his sixteen-page Spurs programme would be full of information about the Nantes players and club. I handed the Nantes programme to Bill. No, it wasn't a ref he knew.

Martin Peters went into the shower room with a ball and started banging it back and forwards against the walls. Eddie Baily moved on from Perryman's thighs to rubbing Gilzean's chest. Johnny Wallis was strapping up ankles. Mike England was putting a new strip of elastoplast on a cut on his forehead. Phil Beal and Mullery were rubbing vaseline on their faces—to stop the sweat going into their eyes during the match. Bill Nicholson went out of the room again. He told Eddie to lock it and let no one in. He'd knock three times to get back. The room was hot and fetid with embrocation. It was more of a crowded concrete cavern than a dressing-room, with no direct light and no ventilation, just a couple of small holes in one corner of the ceiling.

Bill came back, almost bursting the door down in his rage, swearing and cursing. 'They've changed their bloody strip. They told me last week they'd play in yellow. They always play in yellow. That's why they're called the bloody canaries.'

The players tried to look equally concerned and serious. A few joined in the curses, pleased to have something to vent their anger on, an outside body they could all have a go at. Mullery asked why they'd changed their minds.

'For the bloody French TV,' said Nicholson. 'The TV want them to play in green.'

Everyone groaned even louder this time, all cursing TV, saying you should never do anything for those TV cunts. I couldn't see what all the fuss was about. As Spurs were going to play in white, their normal colour, it could make no difference if Nantes played in green as opposed to their normal colour.

'Have you brought any others,' said Nicholson to Johnny Wallis. 'Pat will have to get changed.'

Pat was out at the lavatory. I'd forgotten he always plays in a green jumper. Someone shouted down the corridor for him. When he came back, he was already wearing green. He looked annoyed, when he heard what had happened. Roger handed him a red shirt, to try it on, but Pat said it was OK. He went to his corner and searched around till he found a yellow shirt. He said that would do. Bill went to wash his hands.

Everyone calmed down again, the curses dying out as the talking stopped once again and only the stamping of boots could be heard and the stretching of arms and legs in last minute exercises. Eddie Baily called out the time —fifteen minutes to go. There was a knock at the door and the referee came in, very quickly, catching everyone by surprise. He tapped Pat on the shoulder and pointed to his boots. Pat turned them over to be inspected. He moved on as Pat was holding up his boots, going round the room so quickly, that he hardly seemed to look at more than one pair of boots. Bill tried to grab him as he came round the room and was going out of the door.

'They've changed their shirts,' began Bill. 'It means our goalie is now in yellow, will that be . . .'

But the ref had gone, pushing straight past Nicholson, ignoring him. Bill made a face when he'd gone. The players whistled. 'Not much of an inspection that,' said someone.

'East German, eh,' said Eddie. 'I wonder if he was a POW in the . . .' But he tailed off in mid-sentence, unable to think of a suitable insult.

Bill went to the middle of the room and began addressing his players. They sat silently, each of them taut and gleaming, ready for action. Bill had his head bowed and was moving his hands and arms nervously, walking back and forwards, talking loudly and urgently. There was a feeling of embarrassment, as if the players felt worried on his behalf. They were already completely keyed up. Their minds were on the match. There was only three minutes to go. Nothing he could say now could make much difference, not at this late stage.

'The last time we played in France,' began Bill, 'I know you all remember it. You know what happened. I don't have to go over it. We thought we'd have it easy. But we didn't, did we? I don't want a repeat of that. I want you to go hard, but keep your feet down. Even one foot off the ground and you'll be for it. Don't give that referee any excuses.'

The last time in France had been four years ago at Lyons. Olympique Lyonnais had beaten Spurs 1-0 and went on to knock them out of Europe. That was the night that Mullery was sent off, a night not to remember.

Bill went over a few more points, then finished suddenly. It was as if all he'd been doing was nervously clearing his throat, thinking aloud. His mind was seething with details but he knew that it was too late. He stood in silence, the players watching.

'Now, no arguing with the ref, either,' said Mullery, taking over the silence, becoming keen and captain-like, clapping his hands, moving forward so everyone could see him. 'We've got to go very hard for the first ten minutes. Don't let them get settled. *Hard* all the time. OK lads.'

They were sitting with their heads bowed. A couple of the

reserves exchanged looks as Mullery spoke, quickly, and then looked away. All five reserves were in bulky blue canvas track suits—Roger Morgan, Collins, Daines, Ray Evans and John Pratt. They looked like convicts in a work party.

'One minute to go,' said Eddie Baily. Nobody spoke. It was now like a death cell. As if they were all going out to an execution.

'If you beat this lot,' said Eddie, 'you'll be in the last sixteen. Then after that you'll be in the last sixty-four.'

He was trying to reduce the tension, but as always they were ignoring Eddie's jokes.

'Right, bayonets on,' shouted Eddie as a whistle went in the corridor. 'Over the top. Let's have you!'

They all stood up, stamping their feet, Bill had been busily tidying up the already tidy room as Eddie had been joking. He suddenly beamed and looked expansive and benevolent. As usual, he patted them on the back and wished each one by name the best of luck. Then he went to the shower room where he washed his hands yet again and put on his jacket. He helped Eddie to lock the dressing-room door and then followed the players into the tunnel where they were waiting, lined up, just below the entrance. There was a roar as both teams went out together and a blaze of fireworks lit up the night sky.

The trainers' bench reserved for the Spurs team was just to the left of the centre stand, three wooden forms which we all crowded on to. Just a couple of yards behind us, well within spitting distance, was the crowd, separated by a six foot high wire fence. The crowd were in good temper and gave Bill, Eddie and the Spurs substitutes a cheer as they sat down.

'Get out there,' said Bill, turning to his reserves. 'Get the feel of the turf.' They were a bit embarrassed, not wanting to draw attention to themselves in their baggy blue track suits, only being reserves, but they went out reluctantly to join the first team in white for the pre-match kick around, then they returned hurriedly and sat down. The crowd gave them a derisive cheer. They were screaming in our ears, trying to get us to turn round, shoving beer and bread through the wires, but nobody did. 'Bloody frogs,' said Eddie Baily.

The ball was wet and greasy and from the beginning the Spurs forwards seemed unable to control it. When they tried to collect the ball it bounced off their legs to a Nantes player. When they did get a passing move going, it ended with someone hitting it too far in front. Chivers at last collected a ball well but was robbed before he was ready and gave up without chasing the man who'd robbed him. Eddie screamed abuse. Bill hung his head.

The Nantes team came tearing through the middle right from the beginning, very confident on the ball and in their running. They were doing immaculate wall passes, scattering the Spurs midfield before them, and the crowd was roaring and cheering. For the first half hour, they had it almost all their own way, apart from a couple of isolated raids by Spurs. Even high balls up the middle to the tall Spurs strikers were getting nowhere. Chivers and Gilzean were having no luck. Only Jimmy Neighbour looked dangerous, beating their full backs easily and tearing up the wing, but his centres were not finding their men and he was soon starting to take on one man too many and losing the ball. But he alone looked sharp and on form.

My ears were numb well before half-time. Eddie kept up a continuous stream of abuse, cursing every Spurs mistake when they lost the ball and then screaming orders when the Nantes forwards started thundering towards the Spurs penalty area.

He screamed at Steve to mark number 8, or Gilly to come back, or Jimmy to run wide. He was working himself into a frenzy, yet none of them could hear him. Only when a Spurs player was running down our side of the pitch, right beside us, could his voice be heard. He yelled at Phil Beal, but Phil deliberately ignored him. He yelled at Mullery to urge the team on. Mullery shouted back that he was fucking doing it.

Bill was shouting as well, yelling at Chivers to get moving, but mostly his shouts were sudden blurted-out oaths of panic and fury, burying his face in his hands as once more the Spurs forwards failed to get anywhere. Eddie literally never stopped. His instructions were really a running commentary, shouting out what people should be doing even when he knew they were miles away, hoping by osmosis he might get through to them. Sometimes he just shouted out names, over and over again, screaming at the top of his voice. Sometimes it was sheer gibberish. He jumped on the bench once, putting his knees up in the air, his signal for Chivers to get running, hoping he might be seen by Chivers if not heard. The crowd behind furiously booed and jeered, thinking he wanted Chivers to get the boot in. This wasn't true. Not once did either of them exhort any player to rough stuff. They were concerned with their players getting rid of the ball quickly and intelligently, avoiding bodily contact if

"Gentlemen!
Lanky Alf Padgett, goal scoring mystery man of Ribchester Rangers doesn't exist!"

anything. When a foul was given against Spurs they were furious with their own players for having got into such a position, though it didn't stop them from cursing the ref whenever he seemed to be favouring the opposition.

When it was one of Spurs' three big stars at fault, Eddie was all the more abusive. 'Bloody internationals,' Eddie was screaming. 'Look at them. Play for England but they won't play for us. GET MOVING! DON'T BLOODY STAND THERE! Useless. Too much publicity. It's gone to his head. He won't try any more.'

Half-time came suddenly, in the middle of a stream of Eddie's curses. We followed the players slowly to the dressing-room, letting them get settled. They sat quietly, not looking at each other. Johnny Wallis got some bottles out of a crate which had been left for the Spurs players. It was all Vichy water. There was no tea, which was what the players wanted. They were too limp to be furious. They stared into space, avoiding each other's eyes, hanging their heads, exhausted on their benches.

Bill stood silently for a bit, his face red and contorted, controlling himself as much as possible.

'You're not getting in. You've got to get in first. You're just letting them do those wall passes.'

He went round the defenders individually. He told Mike England and Phil Beal to keep their covering and to watch numbers 7 and 10 breaking through from behind. He said nothing to the forwards. He was furious with them and they knew it. They were furious with themselves, dejected and utterly miserable. Slowly they all started to stand up, looking round, bemused, asking for a drink, looking for some stimulus, some diversion, anything to avoid Bill.

'It's just Fishy water,' said Eddie. 'And there's no bloody glasses either.' I went down the corridor and got some glass coffee cups which was all I could find.

'We don't want any mistakes at the back,' Bill was saying when I returned. 'No silly goals.'

The second half was much the same. Nantes had most of the ball and were still as quick and inventive as ever, especially in midfield. Spurs were sluggish and had no inspiration up front, but the defence was still managing each time to break down the Nantes attack on the edge of the penalty area.

Everyone on the Spurs bench knew that the Spurs forwards were playing badly. It was one of those away games where they seem to hide, to go numb, to stop thinking at the vital moments. Jimmy Neighbour was still trying hard, but Chivers was showing little of his skills. Admittedly he was getting few good balls from his harassed midfield men and not once did the ball bounce his way, but all the same, he made not one chance for himself. You could sense the team praying for him to turn a half-chance into a goal by sheer brilliance and bring himself and the whole team to life.

Gilly was showing a lot of heart, but was getting nowhere. Fifteen minutes before the end, he was brought off and Roger Morgan was sent on, his first appearance in the first team since he'd been injured exactly a year ago. It seemed a rather desperate measure considering he was a long way from being back to first team form, but Bill was obviously hoping for some miracle.

'Do it for us, Roger,' exhorted Eddie, pushing him on.

The reserves stood up to make room for Gilly on the bench. Someone gave him Roger's track suit and helped him to put it on. He sat at the end of the bench, his face shattered with effort, sweat streaming from every pore. Around his head was a halo of steam. He was like a defeated racehorse, frothing and steaming from being pushed almost beyond endurance.

Roger had no chance to show what he could do, though he made one good cross, which was what Bill had told him to do.

Eddie kept up his screams. The crowd behind were now getting angry with him. They'd started by laughing, then had taunted him and now they were furious. They were convinced that he was egging on his players to foul. When Chivers got his name taken, just before the end, Eddie had tomatoes thrown at him from behind.

It was a goal-less draw. Spurs could have scored when Jimmy had a chance towards the end, but it would have been unfair if Nantes had been beaten. They had played well and had the majority of the play. They'd been well drilled, and had run well and intelligently, and their defence had successfully blotted Chivers out of the game. They'd showed none of the inferiority complex about Chivers the local press had led us to believe.

In the dressing-room the players were a mixture of anger, sadness and disappointment. On the way into the tunnel, as we followed the team, a couple of reserves whispered that now we'd see something. Bill would have to say something. No, he wouldn't go for Martin, said one of them. The Big Fellow's now too famous for anyone to criticise him, even on a bad game.

The players collapsed exhausted. Bill stood in the middle, his head bowed, saying nothing.

Martin Chivers was the last to sit down. As he did so he muttered loudly, 'poor team, poor team'. It was a sort of reflex remark, getting in first, as if he expected to be assaulted.

'I never said they were a poor team,' said Bill sharply, looking at Chivers, suddenly angry. 'Never at any time did I tell you they were a poor team.'

Chivers hadn't meant it like that. By criticising them he was really blaming Spurs for not doing better, and himself. He hadn't meant to accuse Bill of misleading them. Bill couldn't have warned them more about Nantes, piling on the details on the strength of their team. In turning on Chivers' remark, Bill was really attacking Chivers, as they both knew.

'They were a poor team,' repeated Chivers sullenly, knowing that Bill had said the opposite. Perhaps he meant that Spurs might have beaten them if they'd been told beforehand they were a poor team. If so, it was a silly line of attack. On the night Spurs had been the poor team.

Chivers was looking for something to say, a way of getting words out, any words, to convey an emotion, a feeling of depression. 'A poor team,' he said again, shaking his head. The lack of logic was a red rag to Bill but he was struggling to control himself.

'You mean *we* had some poor players,' said Bill. He was standing feet apart, shaking slightly, his head up, looking straight at Chivers. He hadn't named any names, but there was no doubt which poor player he was referring to.

'What do you mean,' said Chivers, becoming suddenly violent and animated. Up to now he'd been deliberately sullen, waiting for the real attack to come so that he could plead self-defence.

'What do you know about it? You never praise us when we do well. Never. You never do. What do you know about it? You weren't out there. You didn't have it to do. It's easy to say we didn't do well, bloody easy . . .'

'I've bloody well been out there,' said Bill, determined to finish the argument. 'I know what it's like. I've been through it. What are you talking about? We had some poor players tonight. That's what I'm saying. Some of our players weren't trying. That's what I'm saying.'

'You weren't out there,' continued Chivers, repeating himself once again, but beginning to weaken. It was too early to admit any failings. In his mood of tension, fraught and straight from the field, he was still caught up in his confused mood of bitterness.

Bill waited for him to continue, more than willing to see the argument through, to say to his face what he really wanted to say, but there was a sudden commotion behind him on the table. The anger and the heat and the half-finished fury suddenly began to disintegrate.

Someone had asked for a towel. In throwing a clean one across the table, Eddie Baily accidentally knocked one of the glass cups onto the floor where it shattered, spreading broken glass under the players' bare feet.

Bill left Chivers and got down on the floor and used some soiled tie-ups to sweep the glass under the table out of the way. The players all started talking loudly, jeering at Eddie for his mistake, trooping into the showers to get washed. Soon there were the normal post-match noises and discussions, players showing injuries to Johnny and asking for bandages, going over mistakes

36

made, chances lost.

Chivers didn't move. Everyone else was soon back from the showers and busy putting on their clean clothes, but Chivers sat in his filthy, sweat-sodden, matted strip, just as he'd come from the field. He had one leg across the other, leaning on one elbow, staring straight ahead, menacing, and threatening, yet beaten and fed-up. What's the point. What do I get out of it. Why do I bother. I tried my hardest out there. I wanted to win. I didn't go out there not to try. But that's all I get.

Mullery started singing 'Oh what a beautiful morning' very loudly and badly, knowing he was singing it badly, going right through with all the words, carrying on when people groaned and told him to shut up. After all, it had been a goal-less draw, a good away result. There was the home match still to come.

Someone shouted to Eddie to open the door. They couldn't breathe. The place was like an oven. Eddie unlocked it and opened both doors, swinging them back and forward to make a breeze.

'Close the bloody door,' said Mike England, who was getting dressed just behind the doors. French officials were hanging around outside, trying to stare in. 'They're like monkeys out there.'

'One says open it, one says close,' said Eddie. 'Bloody hell.' He closed both doors and locked them, banging them hard. There was a knock, then another knock,

then another. He opened them furiously, ready to give a mouthful to some monkey. Mr Wale, the chairman, came in, followed by the directors. They crept in rather than walked in, nodding to Bill, not saying anything, sensing the atmosphere, standing demurely against the wall, looking round, talking quietly to each other.

There was another knock and in came Mr Broderick, the Cooks organiser. He went to help Johnny pick up all the dirty clothes and pack the bags— they'd brought a huge canvas holdall this time, not their normal basketwork skips. Bill helped as well, passing over filthy boots and dirty socks. When Bill finished, Mr Wale went into a corner with him where they talked very solemnly.

'The chairman wants you all to go to this reception,' announced Bill apologetically when the directors had trooped out again. 'Don't worry. We'll only stay fifteen minutes. There'll be a buffet there but don't forget there's a meal back at the hotel, if you want it.'

Chivers had started to move at last. He was now in the shower, having peeled off his dirty clothes in a pile at his bench. He'd brightened up a bit, now he'd pushed himself back to life. Bill, Johnny and Broderick were packing away Chivers' dirty strip with the rest of the gear.

Chivers came back to his seat and stood drying himself beside Mike England. 'Did you hear that supporter,' said Chivers. 'Shouting at me I should have scored six.'

'They know nothing,' said Mike, quickly, eagerly. 'They know bloody nothing. I heard one as well. They know nothing.'

'You're right. Nothing at all.'

Mike started gently whistling, quietly and in tune, not a pop song but a piece of Tchaikovsky, from the Nutcracker Suite. He was in his smart three piece suit. He'd washed the vaseline out of his hair and the battle out of his body and he looked like a young managing director about to summon his board of directors.

Some British reporters arrived when the players were ready and were allowed in. They went to Chivers and to Mullery, taking it in turns to talk confidentially in their ears. One had heard the rest of the evening's football results and everyone stopped talking to listen to his news.

On the coach Bill Stevens, Spurs' assistant secretary, was given the job of chucking off the French kids. While it had been waiting, quite a few had crept on and were hiding behind the seats. Chivers was their main target. He signed autographs good humouredly. The bus was surrounded by French fans, waving and smiling. If the crowd felt they'd been robbed by the draw, which is what an English crowd would have thought after a similar performance, they weren't showing it. They were still as fascinated and as pleased to see the Tottenham team, especially Chivers, as they'd been before the match.

The reception was being given by the Mayor of Nantes at the Chateau des Ducs, a towering castle in the middle of the city, with a drawbridge and a wide moat.

It was all lit up when we got there with powdered flunkeys everywhere and a magnificent buffet laid out. The reception was in two large rooms, with a closed circuit TV in the smaller room, so that the guests there wouldn't miss the speeches being made in the other. The Press were also invited, French and British, plus both teams and officials and assorted local dignitaries. Mr Wale and Mr Cox replied in English on behalf of Spurs, thanking the Mayor and people of Nantes for their excellent hospitality, the best they'd experienced in many years of going abroad.

The players stayed about half an hour in all, then Bill said they could go back to their hotel.

Most of them drank lagers in the hotel bar till about one or two o'clock and then went to bed, glad it was all over.

On the plane next morning, only Gilzean was moaning, at least moaning on about France, saying it was his third French trip and he still didn't like it. He preferred any country except France. But the rest were all very cheerful, greatly relieved to be going home, carrying dolls, bottles, souvenirs and other presents.

Champagne was served on the plane, though it was only eleven o'clock in the morning, but I didn't see any of the players drinking it. The directors and the Press managed to have their share.

Chivers was now agreeing he'd had a bad game. He admitted it. He said nothing had gone right for him. He'd been heavily marked and had lashed out in the end out of anger, which had been silly.

Bill Nicholson chatted to a few of the reporters, saying who had had a good game, such as Phil Beal. Jimmy Neighbour had tried hard, he said, though he might have got the ball over more often. He had no praise for Chivers, Peters or Mullery. He nodded towards them as he spoke, not wanting them or the other players to hear.

Later, he told me that he was worried that Chivers was becoming a player who could only play brilliantly at home.

'All they have to do is play it simple. That's the answer, but they won't do it. When you get into difficulties, when the opposing team are doing well and not letting you do anything, all you do is play it very simple till things go your way.'

He opened a newspaper and divided the page in three with his fingers, describing how play could be kept safely in the middle third if things were going badly, even if it meant changing from one flank to another without beating anyone or going forward. He went over passes which had been thrown away. He analysed one move where Peters had tried to pass between two Nantes players and failed when he should have made two simple angle passes.

'I don't know what comes over them. McKay and Blanchflower, they could get a grip when things were going badly, but this team doesn't seem to be able to do it. They've been told often enough what to do. And they *can* do it. I

"Why are you always a sauce bottle during tactical talks?
Because you haven't got the brains to be a cup!"

know they can. I don't know why they don't. It sickens me.'

In the cool clear light of a new day, did he agree with some of Eddie's screams in the heat of the match that some of the players suffered from too much publicity? Surely that couldn't have any effect on their play?

'Players can easily become too confident and arrogant. I don't mind confidence, but it leads to lack of self-criticism. That was what went wrong with some of them last night. They weren't self-critical. Good players like that shouldn't make mistakes, ever. That should be the aim. But if they do make one mistake, that should be it. They should be so furious with themselves that they vow never to do it again. But they won't admit mistakes, so they don't try harder and do better. *Everyone* can do better.

If was a perfect flight, completely different from the dark and the rain and turbulence which we'd had when flying out to the unknown. There was sunshine all the way home and we had a perfect landing at London Airport.

So what can be done, if his players won't do things simply and they won't be self-critical?

'Work at it,' said Bill grimly. 'Work at it. That's all we can do.'

From *The Glory Game*, 1972

FOCUS ON FACT —*The Football Story (5)*   By **Gary Keane & Neville Randall**

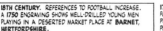

18TH CENTURY. REFERENCES TO FOOTBALL INCREASE. A 1750 ENGRAVING SHOWS WELL-DRILLED YOUNG MEN PLAYING IN A DESERTED MARKET PLACE AT **BARNET, HERTFORDSHIRE**.

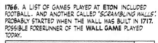

1766. A LIST OF GAMES PLAYED AT **ETON** INCLUDED FOOTBALL. AND ANOTHER CALLED *"SCRAMBLING WALLS"*. PROBABLY STARTED WHEN THE WALL WAS BUILT IN 1717. POSSIBLE FORERUNNER OF THE **WALL GAME** PLAYED TODAY.

1801. **JOSEPH STRUTT**, ANTIQUARY AND NOVELIST, WROTE **"SPORTS AND PASTIMES OF THE PEOPLE OF ENGLAND"**. DESCRIBED FOOTBALL AS A ROUGH AND VICIOUS GAME. *"WHEN THE EXERCISE BECOMES EXCEEDINGLY VIOLENT, THE PLAYERS KICK EACH OTHER'S SHINS."*

FOCUS ON FACT—*The Football Story (6)*   By **Gary Keane & Neville Randall**

19TH CENTURY. MOB FOOTBALL LINGERED ON. IN RURAL DISTRICTS SCHOOLBOYS STILL ROAMED THE FIELDS. PROPELLING A BALL TOWARDS DISTANT GOALS...

...IN TOWNS—LIKE **KINGSTON-ON-THAMES**—YOUTHS STILL TOOK OVER STREETS ON PUBLIC HOLIDAYS. BREAKING SHINS AND WINDOWS. UNTIL SUPPRESSED BY **POLICE** OR MOVED TO RECREATION GROUNDS.

AT **PUBLIC SCHOOLS**, SONS OF THE GENTRY TOOK UP THE GAME. DEVELOPED THEIR OWN VERSIONS DETERMINED BY LOCAL CONDITIONS AND SPACE.

FIRST STEP TO CHANGING MOB AND STREET FOOTBALL INTO AN ORGANISED GAME WITH RULES.

5

Days of Pegasus Past...

Tony Pawson

At Wembley on a Saturday in May, 1974, the 71st and last Amateur Cup final ended a series which began in 1894. Ilford and Bishop's Stortford were somewhat more sophisticated and defensive than the gay cavaliers who met at Richmond 80 years ago, when Old Carthusians beat Casuals 2-1.

Their happy abandon included the late arrival of the Casuals' left back, L.V. Lodge, who missed his train and his side's only goal. Yet Old Carthusians at least would have been in tune with the scientific soccer of the 70's.

Of their victory in the F.A. Cup in 1881, Gibson, the most notable historian of football's early years, wrote: 'If one were asked to say which team deserved to rank as the first scientific one that the football world knew, one must answer the Old Carthusians. There was a magnificent homogeneity about their play, and I believe that they, and not a professional team, first realised the possibilities of combination. The six forwards had learned to subordinate self in the general welfare of the side.'

The six forwards now have shrunk to four, or even two, and none will have the skill of G.O. Smith, who missed the first of Old Carthusians' three finals through selection as England's centre-forward against Scotland. The spirit, too, is now somewhat less carefree. Both finalists come from the Isthmian League, and it would be a matter of astonishment to those Old Carthusians that amateur football should get itself a business sponsorship, or that it needed monetary awards to encourage sportsmanship.

The training might also make the old-timers shudder. Organised preparation was against the amateur concept. Indeed, it was lack of fitness that ended the Old Boys teams' domination of the first decade of the F.A. Cup. When Blackburn Olympic at last defeated Old Etonians in extra time in 1883, Gibson recorded: 'That extra half-hour sealed the fate of the Old Boys. They were quite pumped out, and the Olympic felt the advantage of their week's sojourn at Blackpool. This was the first occasion on which systematic training had been indulged in for the Cup.'

With professionals legalised two years later, it was such training that gave them so decisive an edge in physical fitness and teamwork. Pickford, Gibson's co-writer, recorded that 'that Amateur Cup was started because it had become obvious that the professional clubs were now too strong for amateur sides to compete with, with any hope of getting near the closing stages. Individual amateurs there are at least equal to any professional, but football is a team game, and one brilliant player cannot, like a W.G. Grace, win the match off his own bat.'

Intensive training was thought so unsporting that the Royal Artillery, Portsmouth, were soon disqualified from the Amateur Cup for sending their team to Aldeburgh for a week's training.

Today's approach is closer to the professionals. Bishop's Stortford's manager, Ted Hardy, has in the past taken Dagenham to two finals. When he came to Bishop's Stortford he brought a new approach, and a number of Dagenham's old players. 'What changes did I make? We trained together two evenings a week. Some preferred to train on their own, but discipline is important, and working together is important. I had to sort out a player who thought it was too far to come from Harwich to train.'

The other officials say admiringly of Hardy: 'No one gets many goals against a side Ted manages. If anyone scores against us there is a real inquest into what happened.' Such courts martial are not too frequent, and this defensive skill made Hardy third time lucky, and Bishop's Stortford, in their centenary year, the 36th team to win the Amateur Cup.

When they were due to play Peterborough in the F.A. Cup a season ago, I asked Hardy about the difference between top Isthmian clubs and a League side. 'They're nearly as good as us,' was the curt reply.

Walton and Hersham, the Cup holders, certainly make good that boast when they rendered even Brian Clough speechless by beating his Brighton team 4-0 on their ground. So perhaps this is indeed the appropriate moment to end the distinction.

The trend long evident became brutally clear when Skelmersdale United, led by Steve Heighway, took the Amateur Cup in 1971 and, apparently, payment as well. They were fined £1,000 by the F.A., and turned professional the next season.

The F.A. council's resolution to call all players 'footballers' cannot be passed until September, '74, nor the rules changed until the 1975/'76 season. But the F.A. are acting at once, substituting next season a Vase competition, for which they expect an entry of 240 clubs, while many of the senior amateur sides will enter the Challenge Trophy competition.

42

Two essentials of the Amateur Cup tradition were missing on Saturday. There should surely have been a team from Durham present, for Bishop Auckland are undisputed champions of the competition with 10 wins, while Crook Town are joint runners-up with five.

Nor was there the happy-go-lucky spirit of Mickey Stewart, who gave up an international cap to play in a second round match in 1956. At the time he had no hope of playing if his team reached the final, since he was going on the winter cricket tour to West Indies. But Corinthian Casuals did reach Wembley, and did earn a replay, allowing Stewart to make a 1,000 mile dash home to play. Sadly, he was no Phileas Fogg, and as his taxi drew up at the Middlesborough ground the referee was just whistling the start.

As Ilford, twice winners some 45 years ago, and Bishop's Stortford battled out the last-ever Amateur Cup match, I was thinking of the finals in 1951 and 1953. These were the two that filled Wembley to its 100,000 capacity as our joint Oxford and Cambridge team, Pegasus, brought a touch of romance to the competition. Playing in no league, training together only on their Christmas tour, the Pegasus club, reached the quarter-final in their first season of 1949, to be beaten 4-3 in a marvellous match with Bromley, winners that year of the first Wembley Final.

In their third year, Pegasus won their wings at Wembley, beating the Old Masters, Bishop Auckland, with their captain, Bob Hardisty, the outstanding amateur of his generation. That was also the last year that an amateur, Bill Slater, was to appear in an F.A. Cup Final, in Blackpool's losing team.

For us, the sense of occasion in that packed stadium was as satisfying as for the professionals. Getting to Wembley had been such a distant dream that to be there was happiness. The main memories are of the wall of sound that hammers at you as you emerge from the tunnel with the crowd close on either side. Then Their remoteness once the game starts, and you are no longer aware of them in the intense concentration.

At half-time we were three up against Harwich and Parkeston, and one adviser gave me a swig of whisky, another a ration of rum, and a third a sip of champagne. They improved my swerve, but not all their ministrations could get me to score one of the six goals in the win that rates as the largest, along with the 7-1 defeats of Liverpool Marine by Dulwich Hamlet, and of Stockton by Northern Nomads, or the 6-0 win of Clapton over Eston United.

Pegasus were seen as the essence of amateur football, yet their connections with the professionals were always close and cordial. Vic Buckingham, then Spurs coach, and Billy Nicholson helped to shape the University teams of the time. Buckingham became the Pegasus coach, imbuing us with the tactical ideas that won Spurs the championship in 1951.

When we reached the semifinal, Arthur Rowe sent a telegram: 'Make it simple, make it quick,' and before the final he arranged a practice match against the full Spurs team. That was one of the few special practice sessions we ever had, as a hurried tactics talk when we met on the evening of a match was the usual routine.

Buckingham, articulate and debonair, drew an instant response from the University players. His brief instructions before the final are the only pre-match talk that ever affected me or stayed in my mind. The awe of Bishop Auckland's famous team was dispelled by four simple points. 'Don't worry about what they will do to you, make them worry about what you are going to do to them. Whether you are playing well or badly, *want* the ball all the time. If you can run off the field at the end you won't have given of your best. Win or lose, enjoy the game.'

WANT the ball, ENJOY the game, that really should have been the only advice that amateurs had left to offer the professionals.

From *The Guardian*, 1974

FOCUS ON FACT—*The Football Story (7)*   **By Gary Keane & Neville Randall**

19TH CENTURY. LONDON. CHARTERHOUSE SCHOOLBOYS PLAYED FOOTBALL IN AN OLD MONASTERY CLOISTER 70 YARDS LONG. FORCING THE BALL THROUGH DOORS AT ENDS DEFENDED BY FAGS.
SCRIMMAGES LASTED ¾ HOUR. SHINS WERE HACKED BLUE.

WINCHESTER BOYS PLAYED A DIFFERENT BRAND. BASED ON THE SCRIMMAGE OR "HOT", FROM WHICH THE BALL EMERGED TO BE KICKED DOWN THE FIELD.

1823. RUGBY SCHOOL. A FABLED GAME ON BIGSIDE. WILLIAM WEBB ELLIS, 16, CAUGHT THE BALL IN HIS HANDS, RUSHED FORWARD AND GROUNDED IT BEHIND HIS OPPONENTS' LINE. TO FOUND A BREAKAWAY FOOTBALL— RUGBY.

FOCUS ON FACT—*The Football Story (8)*   **By Gary Keane & Neville Randall**

MID 19TH CENTURY. PUBLIC SCHOOLS DEVELOPED THEIR OWN FOOTBALL GAMES. OLDER SCHOOLS—ETON, HARROW, CHARTERHOUSE, WESTMINSTER— KICKED AND DRIBBLED. NEWER SCHOOLS— CHELTENHAM, MARLBOROUGH, WELLINGTON— ADOPTED RUGBY.

OLD BOYS WENT TO UNIVERSITY, TAKING THEIR FOOTBALL WITH THEM. CAMBRIDGE PLAYERS THRASHED OUT RULES. DRIBBLERS WON. ALLOWED THE BALL TO BE STOPPED BY HAND, BUT NOT CARRIED.

1855-7. SHEFFIELD. OLD BOYS AND YOUNG GRADUATES FORMED THE FIRST FOOTBALL CLUB. WITH RULES BASED ON CAMBRIDGE. TAUGHT LOCAL FOOTBALLERS THEIR KIND OF GAME.
ORGANISED FOOTBALL WAS BORN.

6

Away From It All

Willis Hall

I remember, I remember . . .

I am eight years old. I am wearing a navy-blue swimming cozzie and I am batting for York- shire on golden sands that are hot beneath the soles of my bare feet. The bat and tennis ball have been carefully selected off a Woolworth's sixpenny counter; the stumps consist of a pre- cariously balanced carrier bag and a couple of woolly jumpers. I seem to have been at the crease all afternoon, I am seeing the ball well, smacking boundaries off the back foot in all directions: sometimes as far as a fat man in a deck-chair with a Woodbine packet on his nose, sometimes as far as the edge of the sea. Aus- tralia is represented by dad, bowl- ing medium-pace under-armers, and mum who is long-stop. I seem to remember too that there is a yapping wire-haired terrier fielding in the deep—or is mem- ory playing me false again and I am getting mixed up with the dog that fielded for Lord Snooty and his gang in The Dandy, or was it The Beano . . . ?

We decided to take the kids off to Blackpool for Whitsuntide this year. In doing so, I wasn't only fulfilling a long-felt need to re- live the good life of my early child- hood, I was also going to intro- duce my two lads to the joys of the English seaside holiday. Beach-cricket and beach-foot- ball, that's what seaside holidays are all about; not watching shift- less foreign beach-boys bashing balls with biff-bats on foreign beaches.

'Where's your cricket bat?' I say to my seven year-old, and I glance up from trying to squeeze two quarts of luggage into a pint-sized suitcase.

'What cricket bat?'

'*Your* cricket bat. You know very well what cricket bat. Don't prevaricate. The cricket bat I bought you for your last birth- day.'

He scratches his head, opens his mouth, hangs out his tongue —an irritating habit he has picked up somewhere over the past few months. I am trying to break him of it. 'I got a *Walt Disney Cassette Movie Viewer* for my last birth- day,' he says, eventually.

45

'You also got a very expensive cricket bat,' I tell him slowly, breathing hard, 'with matching stumps. Where is it?'

'Oh, *that* cricket bat,' he says it as if the house was rotten with cricket bats. 'It got broke.'

'Broke? What do you mean, "it got broke"? It can't have got broke. Cricket bats don't *get* broke, somebody breaks them. You haven't played with that bat since the day it came into this house.'

'It didn't get broke playing cricket. It got broke bashing tent pegs in.'

At which point I decide to drop the subject and to buy a new bat once we arrive in Blackpool. After all, I was planning to go on holiday and there seemed little sense in giving myself apoplexy before I'd even got as far as the front gate. I continued to pack in silence and it was the boy who eventually spoke.

'Can I take my *Walt Disney Cassette Movie Viewer* to Blackpool?'

'Certainly not.'

'*Why* not?'

'Because we are packing necessities—not toys.'

'You were going to pack the cricket bat, if it hadn't have got broke.'

'A cricket bat,' I explain, patiently, carefully keeping my voice down, 'is a piece of sporting equipment, it is not a toy.'

'Oh.' He didn't sound all that interested. After a pause, he said: 'Can we take the bagatelle board?'

End of conversation.

I remember, I remember . . .

I am nine years old. I am wearing a pair of grey shorts and a green wolf-cub jersey and I am playing centre-forward for Leeds United on golden sands that are hot beneath the soles of my bare feet. I am the proud possessor of an inflatable beach ball that has travelled with me, annually, to every seaside resort in the North of England, or so it seems. The ball is made of rubber, has alternate blue and green panels, and is dotted with bicycle-tyre repair patches—for I have owned it throughout my entire childhood. I am dribbling down the right wing, past the Gunners' defence. Arsenal consists of my father, who wears braces over an open-necked shirt; and my mother, who is wearing a rose-pink cardigan over a flowered frock and is playing in goal. The blown-up beach-ball clings to my bare instep as if it was fastened there with glue. I side-step and dummy past dad and sprint for goal. I seem to remember, hazily, that the beach-ball once got carried out to sea and that my father was almost drowned in his efforts to rescue it—or is Old Man Memory confusing me again and did that happen to Desperate Dan when an enormous balloon towed him out to Iceland in the Beano, or was it the Dandy... ?

'Where's the football?'

'Which football?' And this time it is my wife who answers.

'My football.'

As is it with cricket bats at our house, so it is with footballs—we are not inundated with the blessed things. But I do happen to own an *Adidas* match-ball. It is mine. It belongs to me. For some reason, it was given to me by Jimmy Hill to celebrate my forty-fourth birthday. It arrived on its own, by taxi, at 8.30 a.m. on that very anniversary of my birth. I have never found out why. We have tried to give it a good home. But I am now forty-five and, to this day, the ball has never been kicked in anger. It has always seemed too good, somehow, to just take outside and punt about the lawn. It is beginning to look sad and to sag in places—ah well, we are none of us getting any younger.

'You are not,' says my good lady, 'intending to take that football to Blackpool?'

'Of course I am. What else?'

'There isn't room for it.'

'We'll *make* room.'

'What for?'

'I intend to teach the lads to play football on the sands.'

'With a real football?'

'Certainly,' I reply, and continue with the wit fairly bubbling out of me: 'I have no intention of travelling with an *unreal* one.'

'People don't play on the sands with real footballs,' she informs me. 'You'll injure someone. They use plastic footballs on the beach.'

Ah, but they do not! They use rubber beach-balls that have alternate blue and green panels and are dotted lovingly with bicycle-tyre repair patches. They dribble for countless hour after hour, through the loose soft sand near the promenade, racing across the hard wet stuff close by the edge of the sea, until it seems as if the ball is attached to their instep and, in their boyhood imagination, they are the heroes of the Victoria ground or Deepdale or Elland Road or, indeed, wherever their fancy lies. Thus it was when Stanley Matthews was a lad and Tom Finney and me.

In the event, I didn't take my match-ball to Blackpool. And, on arrival, I found to my disgust that I couldn't buy a rubber beach-ball with alternate blue and green panels anywhere, much as I tried. I was forced to settle at last for a hideous red and orange inflatable plastic job which, when blown up, looked rather like a damp balloon. It even behaved like one, for every time it was kicked it shot straight up in the air some fifty or sixty feet and hung there for a while like an obscene miniature weather balloon, before floating back to earth, returning inevitably to the exact spot where it had been kicked—either that or the wind took hold of it and carried it along the esplanade. Within an hour, I had made two bus-ride journeys to retrieve the wretched thing.

I did manage to buy a bat, some stumps and a tennis ball though, and we made several abortive attempts to play beach cricket. I think there must have been something wrong with the wicket. When I bowled overarm, the ball left my hand, curved, plopped into the sand and disappeared from view. My four year-old retrieved it with his wooden spade. When I switched to underarm, the ball left my hand, ploughed a shallow furrow through the sand and slowed to a halt some ten yards from the batsman's reach.

Unfortunately, there weren't enough of us in the family to form a quorum for rounders. Disillusionment, coupled with the weather, forced us to give up beach games entirely.

The third day after our arrival, my seven year-old discovered an electronic football machine on the pier. You put in 10p and an electronic white blob of a ball pinged back and forth around a screen while you jiggled a little wheel that controlled an electronic white blob that represented a goalkeeper. The machine gave off an electronic humming noise. The seven year-old became quite proficient at the game; despite his tender years, he seems to have a *penchant* for electronic things. When I was his age, even clockwork motors left me cold and baffled. When I was his age, all pier machines cost a penny, and a pre-decimal one at that.

I am twelve years old. I am wearing a school blazer and my first pair of long flannel trousers. I am standing on tip-toe in order to peer through the narrow eyepiece of a cumbersome pier contrivance on metal legs that is labelled Parisienne Nites. *I turn a handle, slowly at first, and inside the box a stocky lady with tight permed curls begins to take off a long chemise, with jerky movements of her hands, revealing plump white flesh between corset and silk-stocking-top . . .*

Boys will be boys.

There are times when I think I will be glad when my two lads reach puberty. I feel that I shall start to understand them then.

From *Sportsworld*, 1973

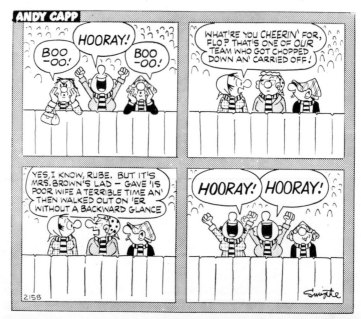

48

7

England v. Portugal

Geoffrey Green

If a rose is a rose is a rose is a rose, then a goal is a goal is a goal is a goal. How much we needed them to enrich Wembley last night when neither England nor Portugal could break what proved to be a stalemate in their European Championship match.

Now England have three points from two games, with home and away ties yet to come against Cyprus, in February and April, and next autumn two away matches against these same Portuguese and Czechoslovakia. By failing to win last night, England have made things harder for themselves and for that have no one else to blame but themselves.

It was a long day's journey into a wet night; a match of low key negatives. The Portuguese, having been beaten easily by Switzerland, now came to Wembley with only one object in mind and that was to escape with a draw. They set about it from the beginning with some hard tackling which stood upon no ceremony; by massed defence; and by adopting offside tactics, a trap which England time after time failed to spring with their high forward lobs.

There were a number of close shaves at the Portuguese end as Damas made two or three last ditch saves—one in particular at the 20th minute when somehow or another, with an elastic leap, he kept out a close-range shot from Thomas after a move down the right flank between Bell, Brooking and Channon. Five minutes from the end, too, he denied the hard-working, probing Channon a chance which he should have taken from Worthington's header to a cross by Thomas. But the quick challenge by Damas smothered the England man at the last stride.

The Portuguese, with Artur, Osvaldinho, Coelho and Alhinho forming a hard core inside their penalty area, achieved what they set out to do, which was to stop England. It worked but it all proved something of a yawn as move after move broke down to become monosyllabic and as monotonous as waves washing the pebbles of a beach. On a night splattered with rain, a whole

D

49

series of implications and significance lay just below the surface.

First Don Revie, having got off on the right foot at the end of the match against Czechoslovakia with a grateful sigh, must now realize how hard the going can be at international level, especially at Wembley, where visitors come these days, it seems, merely to survive with little idea of victory. Secondly, if anyone has to bear the blame for last night's failure it must lie squarely with the midfield men. Francis, Brooking and Todd, for all their individual efforts, failed to unite as a combined force, leaving one to realize that if there is no substitute for skill, there is also no substitute for brain.

All of them, even Thomas, too, and Clarke, seemed to freeze when it came to beating the offside ploy. It is not an easy tactic to undermine, but not once did anybody hold the ball and try to surprise the Portuguese by running through a gap instead of lofting high passes into the area. All this left England's football sadly inhibited as attack tried to fight its damp way past a fast sealing defence which was clever in positional play and short passing.

It was almost from the start that the tragic machinery of the night began to function—from that moment, most significant perhaps, when Damas kept out Thomas when virtually looking at the whites of his eyes. All the near things now matter little. An inventory of them would be a waste of space and time. Suffice it to say that the Portuguese, with one or two quick breaks out of defence, provided moments of danger through their lively front striker, Nene. But for much of the night he, and his forward colleagues, were left like sailors thrown up from a shipwreck on some deserted island while behind them a massed 4-4-2 plan worked its way through the empty night. From the start the fates seemed to be hanging over the wet scene like some uninvited guest.

Perhaps the saddest thing of the whole affair was that the return of Cooper after two years' absence with a broken leg now lasted no more than 25 minutes in an England shirt. Sent spinning in a tackle for a 50-50 ball on a soaking pitch, he left the field injured to find the defence rejigged with the introduction of Todd to the heart of the back four with Hughes again returning to left back, where he had an undistinguished match—not for the first time. This time too, Revie's late substitution of Worthington for Clarke failed to act as the tonic that attended his move in the last stages of the match against Czechoslovakia. These are things the new manager will have to learn to live with.

The England manager said: 'It's very simple, we did not play well at all. You can't have any excuses for that. We didn't deserve any more than a draw. Portugal played well and kept it tight at the back. They were 50 per cent better than when I saw them in Switzerland and tackled harder because this game meant something. The England players are very down in the dumps. They know they didn't play well, but players don't play badly on purpose. We expected the Portuguese to play their defensive tactics. It was up to us to find a way round it and we didn't.

We were not over confident. I stressed to the players we had to treat them with respect. I didn't forecast a hatful of goals, I only said the Portuguese didn't play well against Switzerland.

It was a bad pitch but I'm not looking for excuses. I accept the boos I got at the end as part of the job. The crowd must have been as disappointed as we were', he said. Cooper, said Mr Revie, had injured his Achilles tendon, but he did not think he had been unwise to put him in the team.

ENGLAND: R. Clemence (Liverpool), P. Madeley (Leeds United), D. Watson (Sunderland), E. Hughes (Liverpool), T. Cooper (Leeds United), (sub. C. Todd, Derby County), C. Bell (Manchester City), G. Francis (Queens Park Rangers), T. Brooking (West Ham United), M. Channon (Southampton), A. Clarke (Leeds United), (sub. F. Worthington, Leicester City), D. Thomas (Queens Park Rangers).

PORTUGAL: Damas, Artur, Coelho, Alhinho, Osvaldinho, Octavio, Martins, Alves, Teixeira, Nene, Chico.

Referee: A. Bucheli (Switzerland)

From *The Times*, 1974

FOCUS ON FACT—*The Football Story (9)*   **By Gary Keane & Neville Randall**

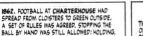

FOCUS ON FACT—*The Football Story (10)*   **By Gary Keane & Neville Randall**

8

Television Coverage

John Bird & John Wells

Opening on the broken-down lavatories of a low-grade football club. We see a television CAMERAMAN, *wearing an anorak, and urinating with his back to us. Julian Period, a TV sports* PRODUCER, *peers round the door of the lavatory.*

PRODUCER: Len—when you're ready—we're coming up to half-time—and we want to get set up for the interview with the manager.

CAMERAMAN: Bloody hell, you don't get time for a pee in this job.

PRODUCER: We've got the camera ready near the trainer's bucket and sponge area, and as soon as he blows up for half-time, I want you to go bang, straight in and sit on his face because it is really live, really off the top of the head stuff and we've only got one shot at it.

We cut to the pitch, and see the CAMERAMAN *and the* PRODUCER *come out of the players' tunnel and cross to an outside broadcast camera where a* SOUND MAN *and the* FOOTBALL MANAGER *are waiting for them. TV cables lead to an*

outside broadcast van.

CAMERAMAN: Can you just mike him up, then we'll be ready to go.

MANAGER: (*Shouting at the match in progress*) That's right, Joe, down the middle: go on Graham, cross it. . . . Oh, you great nellie, get it over. . . . Far post. . . . Gordon, heads!

SOUND MAN: (*Approaching the* MANAGER *with a microphone*) Can I just pop this down your trousers?

PRODUCER: Well, if you're more or less happy, lovie, I'll just pop over to see how it looks on the monitor.

We go with the PRODUCER *as he picks his way over the cables and into the outside broadcast van. With him, we look at a bank of monitors.*

PRODUCER: Right, okay, can you tweak up number one a bit, please?

A whistle blows, on the monitors we see the MANAGER, *still shouting.*

MANAGER: Go on, Tarquin, have a poke, have a poke!

The ball rolls over and stops at the

MANAGER's *feet, he groans and buries his head in his hands.*
PRODUCER : That's the whistle, Cue Manager !
On the monitors we see an interview taking place during the half-time interval, between the MANAGER *and a* TV SPORTS INTERVIEWER.
INTERVIEWER : Well, it's no goals so far, so let's have your live half-time reactions *now !* Wally ?
MANAGER : (*Demented*) All I can say is I feel sick, sick to my stomach. I've sweated my guts out trying to build this team, and look at 'em. They're rubbish, rubbish. If they go on poncing about like a bunch of one-legged fairies in the second half I'll put the whole bloody lot on the transfer list tomorrow morning, and that's a solemn promise. See that Tarquin shooting ? Well, if you're boozing all day and birds all night, what do you expect ? I'll kill him. (*He stumps off*) I'll kill the whole bloody lot of them . . .
We are still with the PRODUCER *who has watched the interview on the monitors inside the outside broadcast van.*
PRODUCER : Absolutely smashing. Knockout. Absolute knockout. Just a tiny problem, he hit his mark fine, but then he drifted a little bit off camera and we lost him : so can we do exactly the same again—tell him it was super, but stay on the mark the whole time and just do exactly what he did then . . .
We go to a TV studio viewing theatre where the PRODUCER, *the* HEAD OF SPORT, *the* EXEC-UTIVE PRODUCER *and the* TV COMPANY ACCOUNTANT *are watching a playback of the afternoon's interview.*
SOUND MAN'S VOICE : Half time interview insert, take five, clock running, five four three . . .
On the TV screen we see the MANAGER's *face, looking stiff and inhibited.*
MANAGER : Well, it's certainly a most interesting encounter, despite the lack of goals : we had our chances, there again, they had theirs. But if we keep spraying it about we have every chance of coming away with at least a draw.
Reactions to the interview on-screen from those assembled in the viewing theatre:
PRODUCER : Wasn't really as fresh as take one.
HEAD OF SPORT : No, with you there : there's a difference, certainly.
PRODUCER : I mean I know the first take was a bit rough camera-wise, but I think that's the one.
The first interview we saw appears on the monitor and freezes on the face of the MANAGER, *mouth open and blurred.*
ACCOUNTANT : There is just the problem. If you look at that closely, we do just glimpse those two . . . what are they called . . . the ones in shorts ?
HEAD OF SPORT : The players, Peter.
ACCOUNTANT : And that would come under the heading of live football as defined in the FIFA/TITS memorandum/wef/August 71. Now of course if we were a news programme we might just

get by that one by a whisker, but as we're a sports programme of course that is totally out of the question. Ha ha ha.

HEAD OF SPORT: All right. I'll come halfway to meet you. Julian, we'll use take two for the pilot.

PRODUCER: But it is over my dead body time, you do realise that?

HEAD OF SPORT: All right, Julian, I'll go along with you on that.

The EXECUTIVE PRODUCER' *dials a number and talks softly in the background.*

EXECUTIVE PRODUCER: Dickie Hart . . . hello?

HEAD OF SPORT: I told you that that man's name will be talked of in every house, club, pub, and television hospitality room in the British Isles. Now what does he say?

EXECUTIVE PRODUCER: Basic-

ally, he's quite keen to do it, provided you see him right with the money.

HEAD OF SPORT: Money, what's he talking about?

EXECUTIVE PRODUCER: Well, he mentioned rather a large figure.

HEAD OF SPORT: What, that little creep? I'll smash his face in.

EXECUTIVE PRODUCER: Well, it's not him it's his agent, actually . . .

HEAD OF SPORT: Agent? Julian, do you know anything about this?

PRODUCER: Well apparently, just after we did the recording he signed up with an agent called Bigg. He said you'd know him.

The HEAD OF SPORT *and the* COMPANY ACCOUNTANT *slowly explode.*

From *Leeds Athletic*, 1974

FOCUS ON FACT—*The Football Story (11)*   **By Gary Keane & Neville Randall**

NOV. 11, 1863. THE NEWLY FORMED F.A. MET TO DRAW UP THE RULES OF FOOTBALL. FIRST DRAFT FOLLOWED CAMBRIDGE AND DRIBBLING SCHOOLS' RULES, WITH TWO EXCEPTIONS... "9. A PLAYER SHALL BE ENTITLED TO RUN WITH THE BALL TOWARDS HIS ADVERSARIES' GOAL"...

"10. IF ANY PLAYER SHALL RUN WITH THE BALL ... ANY PLAYER ON THE OPPOSITE SIDE SHALL BE AT LIBERTY TO CHARGE, HOLD, TRIP OR HACK HIM, OR WREST THE BALL FROM HIM."

DEC. 8. A MAJORITY OF DELEGATES OBJECTED. SUBSTITUTED TWO NEW RULES:- "NO PLAYER SHALL RUN WITH THE BALL. NEITHER TRIPPING NOR HACKING SHALL BE ALLOWED, AND NO PLAYER SHALL USE HIS HANDS TO HOLD OR PUSH."

FOCUS ON FACT—*The Football Story (12)*   **By Gary Keane & Neville Randall**

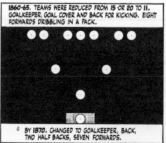

1860s. CLUBS AND SCHOOLS PREFERRING THE DRIBBLING GAME JOINED THE FOOTBALL ASSOCIATION. ADOPTED ITS RULES. PLAYED MATCHES IN JERSEYS AND KNICKERBOCKERS.

FIRST UNOFFICIAL CHAMPIONS: HARROW SCHOOL.

1860-65. TEAMS WERE REDUCED FROM 15 OR 20 TO 11. GOALKEEPER, GOAL COVER AND BACK FOR KICKING. EIGHT FORWARDS DRIBBLING IN A PACK.

BY 1870. CHANGED TO GOALKEEPER, BACK, TWO HALF BACKS, SEVEN FORWARDS.

1875. NORMAL LINE-UP: GOALKEEPER, TWO BACKS, TWO HALF-BACKS, AND SIX FORWARDS REDUCED BY 1885 TO FIVE. HANDLING WAS BARRED.

CLUBS, BEGUN BY OLD PUBLIC SCHOOLBOYS, MULTIPLIED. FOOTBALL, UNDER F.A. RULES, BECAME A NATIONAL GAME. AND A TEST OF MANHOOD.

9

We Are The Champions

Ian Campbell

One more year to waste at school
Fits me for my future role
When I leave the whole world
  knows
I'll join my mates upon the dole

Life holds nothing much for me
Got no future got no dream
When I want to get some action
I come out to watch my team

Then WE ARE THE CHAMPIONS
     Me and all the bovver boys
     WE ARE THE CHAMPIONS
     Get some notice, make
       some noise
     WE ARE THE CHAMPIONS
     We're the rulers of the street
     You'll clear the pavement if
       you're wise
     WE ARE THE CHAMPIONS

We don't fear the boys in blue
There is nothing they can do
They can try to run us in
But we are many, they are few

Older folk make such a fuss
Hoping to influence us
They can stick their good advice
Right where the monkey puts its
  nuts

For WE ARE THE CHAMPIONS
     Me and all the bovver boys

WE ARE THE CHAMPIONS
Get some notice, make
  some noise
WE ARE THE CHAMPIONS
We're the rulers of the street
You'll clear the pavement if
  you're wise
WE ARE THE CHAMPIONS

When we leave the football park
Then we're ready for a lark
Win or lose, our team will know
That we're the boys to make our
  mark

Come on lads, and do your thing
Let off steam and shout and sing
All week long you're nobody
Till Saturday, then you're a king
When
     WE ARE THE CHAMPIONS
     Come on boys, and gather
       round
     WE ARE THE CHAMPIONS
     Terror comes where we are
       found
     WE ARE THE CHAMPIONS
     We're the rulers of the town
     We'll smash it up or tear it
       down
     WE ARE THE CHAMPIONS
     WE ARE THE CHAMPIONS

From *Second House, BBC*, 1974

55

10

Bill Shankly...

Mike Langley

Bill Shankly may have retired but his influence can never clock off until the last Shankly signing, scout, discovery or coach also asks for his pension.

And that, happily, won't be for many seasons because Shankly's successor has the key to Aladdin's cave.

Shankly's legacy isn't only shelves of trophies or titles, or an anthology of soccer laughs. It isn't even the memory of his unique style—that indomitable Scottish optimism, the outrageous comments ('Red Star are a set of pansies') and faith in victory through the sweat-box.

He leaves—as he has been the first to point out—the strongest squad of his fifteen years. Liverpool are already 11-4 favourites for the championship and they'll probably be priced even shorter for the European Cup-winners' Cup.

Everyone has known for a year that Shankly was eyeing the old rocking-chair and speculating about being a full-time grandad instead of being first into Anfield, come rain or fog, at 8.30 each morning.

Yet I believe the power of Liverpool's late challenge last season and the quality of their Cup Final success would keep him hurrying along the trail just one more time.

So apparently did Liverpool's directors, as well as Bill himself. Indeed, everyone except his wife.

For me, Shankly's highest ability lay in his unsentimental assessment of teams and players. It was a sixth sense, even more marked than his talent for dredging up diamonds from the Third Division ashtips.

He knew, before the men themselves, when a player or a side reached the top and was pointing the first toe downhill. To initial gasps of public horror he'd break up good teams—only to construct better ones.

Now his wife Nessie has proved better at the same game. He goes when everyone else wanted him to stay, but would it have been the same in 12 months or two years?

He goes with no debt to football or to Liverpool. We call them a great club today, forgetting that except for losing the 1950 Cup Final and nicking the first post-war championship by a point, their history before Shankly's arrival was 36 years of nothing.

Anfield and Shankly was a marriage made in heaven. He left Huddersfield eagerly for it, saying to his skipper there, Bill McGarry: 'I'm going to a place where they live, eat, sleep and drink football. And that's my place.'

He inherited a set of Second Division heavyweights I remember describing as 'more likely to win a tug-of-war than promotion.'

But Bill got them up in a couple of years, by dynamism, by encouragement, by such unbounded enthusiasm that Ray Wilson, the old England left-back, says: 'You felt he was the only manager in the world who might spend his own money to buy a player.'

Denis Law, whom Shankly had coached as an amateur at Huddersfield and Wilson, whom he left behind there, are possibly the only two great players of his 25 years in management.

Admirers of Roger Hunt, Ian St John and Kevin Keegan are entitled to differ but, by the most stringent tests of greatness, think only Law and Wilson qualify.

Liverpool under Shankly won three championships, two F.A. Cups, the E.U.F.A. Cup and the Second Division title with the absence of great players concealed in superb but system-built teams.

But they had a great manager and the greatest crowd. I make no apologies for retelling former chief scout Norman Low's wonderful story of Shankly's feeling for the Kop.

'The phone went a few days before the Cup Final against

"Their substitute's warming up .... Get him."

Leeds. Bill picked it up and I could hear a Brummagem accent, a real yow-yow, on the other end.

'Bill says, "Yes, yes, what do you want, sir?"

'The fellow said, "Did you get my letter?"

'"What letter, would it be after tickets."

'"Yes, I wrote to you from Birmingham."

'Bill exploded: "Birmingham, Birmingham? You know what, sir, you know what—I've got a hundred relatives and there's not one of those beggars getting a ticket.

'"They are going to the boys on the Kop, any tickets I've got.

'"By Christ—BIRMINGHAM, BIRMINGHAM!"'

If there is a Shankly testimonial, the Kop will guarantee to fill Anfield twice over. Neither they nor football can forget him, but they're wrong if imagining his like will never be seen again.

Somewhere out on the cinder-track circuits of Workington, Carlisle, Grimsby and Huddersfield, where Shankly spent 12 years learning his business, there must be another extraordinary extrovert with head and heart full of football. And able, in victory or defeat, to make us laugh.

But neither Liverpool nor anyone else will get him for what Shankly signed in 1959—£50 a week and no contract.

From the *Sunday People*, 1974

FOCUS ON FACT—*The Football Story (13)*   By Gary Keane & Neville Randall

1867. GLASGOW. SPORTING GENTLEMEN MET TO FORM QUEEN'S PARK FOOTBALL CLUB. PLAYED MATCHES IN SUMMER AGAINST OTHER EMERGING SCOTTISH CLUBS: THISTLE, HAMILTON GYMNASIUM AND AIRDRIE.

1870. C.W. ALCOCK, F.A. HON. SEC., PROPOSED "AN ANNUAL TRIAL OF SKILL BETWEEN THE CHAMPIONS OF ENGLAND AND SCOTLAND."

NOV. 19. TEAMS CHOSEN FROM OLD BOY AND UNIVERSITY CLUBS MET AT THE OVAL. ENGLAND WON 1-0. INTERNATIONAL FOOTBALL WAS BORN.

1870. BRITONS IN HAMBURG AND BREMEN STARTED FOOTBALL THERE. 1875. OXFORD UNIVERSITY MADE THE FIRST OVERSEAS FOOTBALL TOUR TO ENCOURAGE THEM. GERMAN UNIVERSITY AND CLUB TEAMS WERE FORMED.

FOOTBALL WAS BECOMING INTERNATIONAL.

FOCUS ON FACT—*The Football Story (14)*   By Gary Keane & Neville Randall

1871. LONDON. AN F.A. COMMITTEE MEETING. CHARLES ALCOCK MOVED A MOTION.

"IT IS DESIRABLE THAT A CHALLENGE CUP BE ESTABLISHED... FOR WHICH ALL CLUBS BELONGING TO THE ASSOCIATION SHOULD BE INVITED TO COMPETE."

1872. A SILVER CUP WAS BOUGHT FOR £20. (LATER STOLEN AND REPLACED). 15 TEAMS ENTERED. QUEEN'S PARK FROM GLASGOW, DONINGTON GRAMMAR SCHOOL, LINCOLNSHIRE. AND 13 AMATEUR CLUBS IN LONDON AND THE SOUTH-EAST.

QUEEN'S PARK DREW WITH WANDERERS, EX-PUBLIC SCHOOLBOY TEAM IN THE SEMI-FINAL. RETURNED TO SCOTLAND THROUGH LACK OF FUNDS. 2,000 SPECTATORS, AT 1s. A HEAD, SAW WANDERERS BEAT ROYAL ENGINEERS—ALL OFFICERS—IN THE FINAL AT THE OVAL 1-0.

11

...And His Wife

Jane Gaskell

'Between you and me, love,' says Nessie Shankly, 'it's just for me that Bill has announced his retirement. He knew the tension and strain of being married to Liverpool's manager was getting me down.'

Agnes Shankly, married thirty four years to one of football's most formidable giants, is talking in her neat living room—looking out on the spotless little garden in which Bill Shankly will be spending a lot of time now.

'I'd had it up to here.' Nessie indicates her cotton blouse neck. 'When he stayed away from the World Cup it was because I was unwell. I know people wondered about Bill's health—oh, no,' she explains.

'Bill is as fit as a fiddle! He trains even in the close season. He goes off regularly to do his little bit of training and has a sauna. Of course he's tired—you can be as fit as a fiddle, love, and still be tired.

'You can reach a pitch when you say, "That's it! I've had enough."

'And that's what I've said, you see. When Liverpool were playing in the Cup, I was as you see . . .' Nessie Shankly holds out a hand with a tiny tremble. 'I was highly strung and full of tension.

'*Saturdays when they were playing, whether Bill was here or away, were terrible. Bill gives so much of himself. Anyone with him has to feel for him, and with him.*'

This morning Nessie will as usual come downstairs to eat the breakfast her husband has already cooked: Tea, toast, marmalade, maybe a boiled egg. But it will probably be later than usual.

'He will go to the ground to keep things going a bit,' she says, 'but there'll be no need to be there every day at the same time any more. He is usually there by 8.30—but perhaps now we can have a lie-in in the mornings.'

Nessie again looks out at the garden, where early every morning four green parrots with orange beaks swoop down on the nuts Bill leaves out for them. 'We don't know where they come from,' she says.

'One thing is certain,' she stresses. 'We'll not leave Liverpool. We love the place. And it has given us all its love. The people here are warm.

'Besides, all our family is here. Our daughter, Barbara, is married to a Liverpool policeman.'

At the family conference at which Shankly's resignation was decided, his three grandchildren were taken into consideration. They are his daughter Barbara's three little girls.

They hardly ever see him except for family dinner on Sundays. But Karen, nine, Pauline, eight, and Emma Jane, all of 22 months, love the stories their famous grandfather tells them about when he was a boy and didn't have what they have now.

'I can't imagine him as a miner,' says Nessie. 'But he was born in an Ayrshire mining village, so there was nothing else for it. Now the grandchildren will see more of him.'

So will the roses. There are plenty to prune. The Shanklys say they're home birds and they'll watch television ('Not these stupid things with no good story,' says Nessie, 'but we've been enjoying *Sam*. That's about miners'). But Nessie Shankly still won't dare ask him to take her out to a show.

'I'd really love it!' Her face lights up.

'There's the corny old story of how a friend met us both coming out of a little Fourth Division match. Everyone knows I don't like or understand football, so he

was surprised. Bill said: "Well, it's her birthday! I took her out for a treat!"'

Nessie loved him when they first met during the war at the Bishopsbriggs RAF station outside Glasgow. Nessie, a Glaswegian, was a Waaf, Bill an airman.

'He never did beat about the bush,' she says ardently. 'Everything comes straight from the shoulder with him. Once its off his chest, and it's said, he doesn't bear a grudge.'

Nessie pauses, her pretty blue eyes quite sad. She says again: 'Bill has resigned for my sake. Football has been his life.

'*I still don't even know the rules. I always felt there was no point in going. I always felt if I went to a match I'd be keeping someone else out of a seat.*

'My daughters (Barbara 29, Jeanette, 23) are not interested either. I've brought them up right!' Nessie jokes.

She doesn't know if he'll have the patience for retirement. She says she's a Scrabble addict—but when she tried it out with him once, he soon gave up.

'I've never really pushed him,' says Bill Shankly's wife. 'I've always been behind any decision he made.

'But last year this was something I asked him. I wanted him to think about retirement. And this month he really did think about it, didn't he, love?'

From the *Daily Mail*, 1974

12

As She Is Spoken

Argentine F. A.

This ten World Championship to begin at Federal German Republic, that which will make the whole world a great game-camp and will make vibrated in a 'goal' cry all countries football lovers, during more than twenty days, will have by sixth time Argentine representatives participation.

Because of that the Argentine Football Association knowing its own population and sportsmen feelings from the team that which will play at Federal German Republic, has the pleasure in sending to the West German Football Federation Organising Committee, to FIFA authorities, to all final participating delegations and to every football lover, a kindly greeting and a friendship feeling.

Our Argentine, 1978 World Championship seat. Is ready to open doors to keep gladly every sportsman brother to get the final object: conquer from sport the brotherly unity of the whole world.

From an *Argentine FA handout*, West Germany, 1974

"I've got a feeling he's on our wanted list ..."

13

Double Tops

A.J. Ayer

It has been done at last. For the first time in this century a single team has won 'the double'—both the Football League Championship and the F.A. Cup. Arsenal came near it in the thirties; Manchester United looked almost certain to achieve it four seasons ago; Wolverhampton Wanderers, who won the cup last year, were within a point of heading the league. Last Saturday Tottenham Hotspur brought it off. They had already won the League championship with a total of points which equalled the record set up by Arsenal thirty years ago; they had achieved the record number of wins in the League, including a record run of eleven matches at the opening of the season; their performance in away matches had given them yet another record. By defeating Burnley in the semi-final they had eliminated their most dangerous rivals for the cup. Leicester City whom they had to meet in the final were quite a formidable team. In League matches, the Spurs had beaten them at Leicester, they had lost to them at home; in fact, Lei-cester were the first team to win at Tottenham this season. Nevertheless, the experts almost unanimously picked the Spurs to win.

The experts were right. The Spurs did win by two goals to nothing, but though a famous, it was not a magnificent victory. On the day, as one of the Leicester players said a little sourly after the match, the Spurs were not 'super'. There have been many occasions this season when the Tottenham cock has had better reason to crow. They were not noticeably nervous, but they did seem rather jaded. The strain of living up to their reputation throughout the long league programme had taken its toll of them. Blanchflower, their right-half and captain, who more than anyone has been responsible for the team's success, looked a little tired; Mackay, the other wing-half, lacked something of his usual drive; the inside-forwards, White and Allen, were both a little out of touch. In fact, the Spurs owed their victory mainly to what some critics had thought to be their only possible weakness, their defence. In particular, their left-back, Henry, played a superb game. On this form, he deserves to play for England; it can only be the reluctance of the England selectors to disturb a winning team that keeps him out of the World Cup.

The Spurs lost the championship last season, when they seemed to have it won, because their mid-field play was let down by their finishing; they made the openings but failed to score the goals. This is an old fault of theirs, which even in this triumphant season has occasionally cost them matches that they could have won. For a long time on Saturday it looked as if this was again going to be their downfall. One wondered if a goal would ever come. White missed an easy chance in the opening minutes; just before half-time Jones had what seemed to be a good goal disallowed for off-side; Allen and Dyson missed open goals in the second half. It was not until the last quarter of the game that Smith, the centre-forward, beat a Leicester defender skilfully on the turn and scored with a shot which the goalkeeper had no chance to save. This goal was decisive. The Spurs belatedly took charge of the game, and it was no surprise when the left-winger, Dyson, headed a second goal to make their victory complete.

The greatest fear of the Spurs' supporters before the game had been that an injury at Wembley would rob their team of the double; as it did Manchester United four years ago. In the event, the game was marred by injury, but by an injury to one of the Leicester players. After less than twenty minutes, the Leicester right-back, Chalmers, hurt his leg in a tackle; he stayed bravely on the field, but was only a passenger at outside-left. For more than three-quarters of the game the Leicester side was practically reduced to ten men. Under this handicap, they played extremely well. Banks in goal, McLintock, the right-half who took Chalmers' place at back, and King, the centre-half were outstanding; but the whole defence was resolute, and the forwards often threatened to break through, especially in the opening period of the second half. Leicester are not a conspicuously artistic side, but they are strong and fit and thrustful, in the tradition of midland English football. If, as is probable, they deputize for Spurs in the European Cup-Winners' Cup next season, since the Spurs as League Champions will be competing in the European Cup, and can hardly manage both, they should do very well.

It is idle to speculate what would have happened if Chalmers had not been injured. What can be said is that it is intolerable that the Cup Final should be vitiated year after year by injuries of this kind. This is surely an occasion on which it should be allowed to introduce substitutes, as it already is in many international matches, at least up to half time. There would have to be safeguards to prevent abuses, but they should not be very hard to devise.

How good is this Spurs side? Are they the team of the century, in merit as well as in achievement? By the very highest standards, they are not a team of stars. Blanchflower is a very great player, at his zenith the best wing-half that I have ever seen, but he is nearing the end of his career. Of the others only Jones, a wing-forward with the speed and swerve of a rugby three-quarter, could clearly command a place in a current world eleven. Of course they have good players besides these. Norman is a dominating centre-half. Mackay can play like a tornado. Though White is erratic, his intelligent play at inside-forward has won the team many of its matches; he has the positional sense of a great player. Smith, who is now the England centre-forward, has played better this year than he ever has before. He is a clumsy-looking footballer, and there are periods when nothing will go right for him, but he has more skill than one might think and he rises splendidly to an occasion. In the semi-final as well as in the final of the Cup, and in the critical league match with Sheffield Wednesday, which settled the championship for the Spurs, it was his well-taken goals that turned the scale.

Nevertheless, it is not so much to the individual merits of the players as to their team work

"Attention please, we have reason to believe that a dangerous lunatic is in the ground."

that the Spurs owe their extraordinary success. They have kept very nearly the same side for two seasons, and they have in this season been very little disturbed by injuries. The result is that they have achieved a remarkable understanding. In their use of the open space, they resemble the famous Spurs team which won the league championship ten years ago. But whereas the 1950 eleven relied, under Arthur Rowe's management, exclusively on 'push-and-run', a style which is very beautiful to watch when it is successful but one which makes very heavy demands upon the players' energy, the present team has been able to blend this 'continental' style with the English long-passing method. One of their most considerable achievements has been their ability to pace a game, to conserve their energy between bouts of pressure: it has repeatedly brought them goals in quick succession. For this they owe much to their manager, Bill Nicholson, who was himself a member of the 1950 team, but still more, I think, to their captain, Danny Blanchflower, whose control of them on the field has always been intelligent and sure. At their best, I think they have been superior to any English team since the war, though the Manchester United side, which was broken by the Munich air crash, ran them very close. I am not sure that they are better than the great Arsenal sides of the thirties, though it is perhaps in their favour that the game is probably played nowadays at a faster pace.

How will they fare next season in the European Cup? A fast, hard-tackling side like some of the West German teams might throw them out of their rhythm. Against a team of artists like Real Madrid, their own artistry should flourish. I cannot wager that they will beat Real Madrid; but if at any stage they are drawn against them, it should be a wonderful game to watch.

From the *New Statesman*, 1961

FOCUS ON FACT—*The Football Story (15)*   **By Gary Keane & Neville Randall**

1870s. UPPER-CLASS TEAMS DOMINATED. CUP WINNERS INCLUDED OXFORD UNIVERSITY, OLD ETONIANS, AND OLD CARTHUSIANS.

NEW RULES ADDED CORNER KICKS AND ALLOWED GOALKEEPERS TO HANDLE.

1874. NORTHERN AND MIDLAND INDUSTRIAL WORKERS BEGAN TO PLAY. BIRMINGHAM WESLEYANS, WITH HELP FROM MIGRANT SCOTS, FORMED A CLUB CALLED ASTON VILLA.

TWO OLD BOYS FROM BLACKBURN GRAMMAR SCHOOL FORMED BLACKBURN ROVERS.

1878. RAILWAYS BROUGHT SPECTATORS TO IMPORTANT MATCHES. ON *OCT. 14*, AT BRAMALL LANE, SHEFFIELD, A MATCH WAS PLAYED UNDER NEWLY-INVENTED ELECTRIC LAMPS. FIRST FLOODLIT FOOTBALL.

E

14

Kicking The Habit

Ian Davies

'Got any fag cards, mister?'—it was a familiar cry which followed most smokers in pre-war days, usually just as the smoker was about to throw away an empty packet in the street. It was the pre-Womble era when depositing litter hardly raised an eyebrow.

Except, that is, to a rabble of little boys reminiscent of those accosting voyagers embarking at Bombay or Port Said. They were not, however, after alms or a few annas. Their quest in this case was some of those small cards contained in every packet of cigarettes.

They measured $1\frac{7}{16}$ in. by $2\frac{11}{16}$ in. (38mm x 68mm), usually in sets of 50, each set being a collection of information about a certain subject. That they influenced smoking habits there is no doubt. A smoker might change his brand—perhaps from one currently featuring 'Flags of the British Empire' or 'How to Play Lawn Tennis' to 'In Your Garden' or 'British Naval Ships'.

There was a strong sporting influence. It started with cricket in late Victorian times when cricket dominated British sport. W.G. Grace, Ranjitsinhji, C.B. Fry— they all appeared, and cricket remains the most popular cigarette-card sport. In the Memorial Museum at Lords', most of the outstanding cricketers from Grace to Compton, D. appear in cigarette-card form.

Football, too, was well represented, and the value of the biographical notes to the football historian is incalculable. From 1920 to 1939 only one English international did not appear on a cigarette card. He is Walter Alsford of Tottenham Hotspur who played for England against Scotland in 1935.

Most Scottish, Irish and Welsh internationals are also prominent, and some of the detail on the reverse side of the card is hard to find in any football reference book. Illustrations vary—from rough line-drawings in colour, through quite distinctly detailed portraits, to one magnificent set, issued by John Sinclair, of Newcastle, which show their subjects in actual photographs. There are two series featuring the work of the two outstanding cartoonists of their day—Rip and Mac.

A familiar figure, still quite recognisable 40 years on, carries this biography on the back : 'Born in Glenbuck, a notable Ayrshire nursery for footballers, — is a member of a family of whom five have played first class football. From Glenbuck Cherrypickers he went to Carlisle in 1932 and a year later a big career opened for him with Preston North End. He appeared in the 1937 and 1938 cup finals obtaining a winner's medal in the latter year against Huddersfield. Also in 1938 he was Scotland's right half against England. A player who joins traditional Scottish craft with wonderful stamina, he has since played in four more representative matches.'

A similar card now would have told you that today he is manager of Liverpool and his name is William Shankly. On another card, part of his 'well-known footballer' brother, Bob, is featured— a rather crude illustration this, consisting of a photographic head on a cartooned body.

The most popular subject in the footballers' series is Stanley Matthews, who appears in every set from 1934. In his first appearance—in that year—he is described as 'showing consistent form on the right wing for Stoke City.' And in the last football series he has become 'a wing forward of unsurpassed brilliance.'

This description is rather more favourable than usual. The biographies normally stick to the facts, although Wilf Mannion, of Middlesbrough, is described as 'one of the most notable discoveries in modern football.'

Another one must have been Eric Stephenson, the pre-war Leeds and England forward. We are told about his initiative, and also that he was a captain in the Boys' Brigade—a hint perhaps of the qualities that won him a posthumous Military Cross while fighting the Japanese in Burma. He was then an Army major.

The cigarette firms were always quick to spot the potentially great. Tommy Lawton became the subject of a card shortly after joining

FOCUS ON FACT —*The Football Story (16)*

By Gary Keane & Neville Randall

1878. F.A. CUP FOURTH ROUND. FAVOURITES, OLD ETONIANS, MET A TEAM OF MILL WORKERS FROM DARWEN, LANCASHIRE, WERE HELD TO A 5-5 DRAW.

TOOK TWO REPLAYS TO BEAT THEM. WENT ON TO WIN THE FINAL.

1881-2. ANOTHER MILL TOWN TEAM, BLACKBURN ROVERS, REACHED THE FINAL. TO LOSE 0-1 TO THE OLD ETONIANS. THE OLD BOYS LAST WIN. NEXT YEAR, ANOTHER LANCASHIRE TEAM, BLACKBURN OLYMPIC, BEAT OLD ETONIANS IN THE FINAL 2-1.

NEXT THREE YEARS. BLACKBURN ROVERS WON THE CUP — THREE TIMES IN A ROW. THEY HAD BEATEN THE PUBLIC SCHOOLS AT THEIR OWN GAME. THE ERA OF NORTHERN WORKING CLASS — SOON PROFESSIONAL — SUPREMACY WAS BORN.

Everton at the age of seventeen. Just how well he was known can be gauged from the fact that the producers, Churchmans, had his initial wrong, and he appears as J. Lawton who 'has developed the exceptional talents he showed as a schoolboy.'

Personal details abound. We learn that W. Hughes of Birmingham is a teetotaller and an enthusiastic walker, that Frank Broome was told he was too small by every other club except Aston Villa; that opponents said of George Mason, of Coventry, 'Keep the ball away from Mason' (they omit to say why).

Other information invaluable to opposing teams includes: Norman Dinsdale (Notts County)—'Dinsdale takes his football very seriously'; George Male (Arsenal) —'Is notable for his fine positional play'; Bobby Gurney (Sunderland)—'He has a trick of going out to the wing and crossing the ball quickly, a move which has produced many goals.' (Not many more after *that* card was published!)

But Thomas Watson of Cardiff City owes much to his cigarette card biographer. 'His timing of a tackle sends the old campaigners in the stands into ecstacies. His calm-eyed consistency was a decisive factor in Cardiff's success.' You can't say fairer than that— except that something went wrong, because Cardiff were relegated that season!

The war brought an end to cigarette cards, but not to collecting them. It is a hobby that flourishes, and, as with every other collecting hobby, values rise. An immediately pre-war series of 'Association Footballers' can cost as little as 48p. But '150 Footballers', issued in 1914, will cost you a mere £75.

From *Sportsworld*, 1974

15

Stanley Matthews

Alan Ross

Not often *con brio*, but *andante,
andante,* horseless, though
jockey-like and jaunty
Straddling the touchline, live
margin not out of the game,
nor quite in,
Made by him green and magnetic,
stroller
Indifferent as a cat dissembling,
rolling
A little as on a deck, till the mouse,
the ball, slides palely to him,
And shyly almost, with depreca-
tory cough, he is off.

Head of a Perugino, with faint
flare
Of the nostrils, as though,
Lipizzaner-like, he sniffed at
the air,
Finding it good beneath him, he
draws
Defenders towards him, the ball a
bait
They refuse like a poisoned choc-
olate, retreating, till he slows his
gait
To a walk, inviting the tackle,
inciting it

Till, unrefusable, dangling the ball
at the instep
He is charged—and stiffening so

slowly
It is barely perceptible, he exe-
cutes with a squirm
Of the hips, a twist more suggest-
ive than apparent, that lazily
disdainful move *toreos* term a
Veronica—it's enough.
Only emptiness following him,
pursuing some scent
Of his own, he weaves in towards,
not away from, fresh tacklers,
Who, turning about to gain time,
are by him harried, pursued not
pursuers.

Now gathers speed, nursing the
ball as he cruises,
Eyes judging distance, noting the
gaps, the spaces
Vital for colleagues to move to,
slowing a trace,
As from Vivaldi to Dibdin,
pausing, and leusurely, leis-
urely, swings
To the left upright his centre, on
hips
His hands, observing the goalkeeper's spring, heads rising
vainly to the ball's curve
Just as it's plucked from them;
and dispassionately
Back to his mark he trots,
whistling through closed lips.

69

Trim as a yacht, with similar
  lightness—of keel, of reaction
  to surface—with salt air
Tanned, this incomparable player,
  in decline fair to look at, nor in
  decline either,
Improving like wine with age,
  has come far—born to one, a
  barber, who boxed
Not with such filial magnificence,
  but well.

'The greatest of all time,'
  meraviglioso Matthews—Stoke
  City, Blackpool and England.
Expressionless enchanter, weav-
  ing as on strings Conceptual
  patterns to a private music,
  heard
Only by him, to whose slowly
  emerging theme He rehearses
  steps, soloist in compulsions
  of a dream.

16

Manchester United Disaster

H.E. Bates

Late on a cold February afternoon of this year I was driving home from London when I suddenly saw, under the first lighted street lamps, one of those blue and yellow news placards that are designed so often to shock you into buying a newspaper you don't particularly want and that, nine times out of ten, you would be just as well without.

'Manchester United In Air Crash', it said. My immediate reaction was, I confess, a mildly cynical one. The announcement seemed to me to belong to pre-precisely the same category as 'Winston Churchill in Car Crash' —the car crash almost invariably turning out to be nothing more than a tender argument between the starting handle of an ancient Austin Seven and the great man's Rolls-Royce somewhere in the region of Parliament Square. I am getting too old, I thought, to be caught by newspaper screamers.

At six o'clock, out of pure curiosity, I turned on my television set. As the news came on, the screen seemed to go black. The normally urbane voice of the announcer seemed to turn into a sledge-hammer. My eyes went deathly cold and I sat listening with a frozen brain to that cruel and shocking list of casualties that was now to give to the despised word Munich an even sadder meaning than it had acquired on a day before the war when a British Prime Minister had come home to London, waving a pitiful piece of paper, and most of us knew that new calamities of war were inevitable.

Roger Byrne, Bill Whelan, Duncan Edwards, Tommy Taylor, David Pegg, Geoff Bent, Mark Jones, Eddie Colman—of Manchester United's flashing young giants hardly one had been out of the cradle at the time of the first Munich disaster. Probably not one of them had kicked a football in that year on the eve of the war when England had sent to Berlin eleven other giants to thrash the team representing Hitler's master-race by six goals to three.

By the time war was over it was inevitable that the heroes of that resounding Berlin victory—men like Tommy Lawton, Raich Carter,

Wilf Copping, and Stan Cullis—were on the verge of slipping from the international football scene. A new race of giants had to be found to represent the country that had taught the rest of the world all that was best in the skill and beauty of soccer. And soon, as men like Carter, Drake, Lawton and Cullis turned their talents to the tutorship of new teams, we began to hear more and more of a man, up in Manchester, who appeared to be dedicated to the apparently revolutionary notion that you can make mature footballers out of boys in their teens.

To me that idea of Matt Busby's never seemed in the least bit extraordinary. There is nothing more true about football than that it is a young man's game. In youth the eyes have a fantastic swiftness, limbs are marvellously supple, with powers of resilience, and recovery unknown later. The clay of young flesh is a beautifully plastic thing that can be trained and shaped under skilled teaching in endless and remarkable ways. Not only in football has the principle of shaping extreme youth proved to be an excellent one. Who, twenty years ago, would have dreamed of swimmers of thirteen and fourteen representing their native countries and breaking world records? Today these things are commonplace.

Gradually, as the Busby principle of teaching was translated into reality, the names of the top students began to emerge. We began to hear of players representing Manchester United in the First Division at the age of seventeen. Presently we were to see the greatest of all the Busby prodigies, Duncan Edwards, an appealing giant of a boy, representing England at the age of eighteen, striding the Wembley pitch like a mature colossus, gaining the first of his eighteen international caps, under each of which he increased in stature so much that at twenty-one he was not only a veteran but clearly England's future captain.

If I select Duncan Edwards as the most compelling of all the young Manchester men who will now never play football again it is because he always seemed to me the epitome of all that was best in skill and character in the team that became popularly known—and very foolishly I think—as the 'Busby Babes'. I have always intensely disliked that cheap journalistic label and I have a fancy that most of the players may have done so too. There was certainly nothing of a babe about Edwards. A more mature young man, both in physical strength and artistry, never walked on to that treacherous and difficult turf at Wembley to play for his country.

You could say almost the same of that excellent and cultured back Roger Byrne, who gained thirty-three England caps; of the energetic and enthusiastic Tommy Taylor; and of Pegg, Colman and Jones, all of whom, like Duncan Edwards, had been schoolboy stars ; of Whelan, who also appeared for his native Ireland, and Bent who travelled to Belgrade as a reserve. Footballers, George Bernard Shaw once said, have their brains in their feet, but I have always had a sneaking notion that Matt Busby liked to be sure that his young men had a few brains in their heads too.

But what these young prodigies possessed above all, I think, was class. It is an attribute not easy to define, but when Manchester United were beaten in the 1957 Cup Final by an Aston Villa playing very robust but not very good football, it was also pure class that made them, I think, as admirable in defeat as they had so often been in victory. And when they were again and deservedly beaten in the 1958 Cup Final it was not merely because they were lacking in the necessary arts and skills. The class was not there.

And how could it possibly have been ? Its ashes lay irreparably scattered across a German airfield after the cruellest day in English sporting history. Whether the same degree of class will ever be seen again in the United colours it is too early to tell ; but one thing is certain. If it never returns it will not be the fault of Matt Busby, the tutor, happily still with us ; or of the young men to whom, so very early in life, he taught the beauties of our national game, and who, having acquired fame in youth, set such an adult example before they were so prematurely and tragically taken from the field.

From the *FA Year Book*, 1958

FOCUS ON FACT —*The Football Story (17)*   **By Gary Keane & Neville Randall**

FOCUS ON FACT —*The Football Story (18)*   **By Gary Keane & Neville Randall**

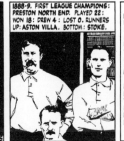

17

Religious Fervour

Peter Terson

(*Enter a football fan vicar*)
VICAR:
I am the football fan vicar,
This is where my congregation
  stands.
Listen to their hymns of praise
And hymns of glory.
This is where the sermon must
  take place,
Not in an empty church
With an empty story.
Jesus wasn't a hermit, wasn't a
  square,
His pulpit was where people
  were.
Wherever he went there was a
  great assembly.
I say that in the modern age
Jesus would have taught at
  Wembley
The sermon on the Mount
The Parables of the Wine, and
  Fishes.
To teach and preach at Anfield
  Park,
St James, the Victoria Ground,
Ninian Arms Park, and Craven
  Cottage
Would be his wish.
Don't talk to me about rowdyism,
Vandalism, hooliganism.
Out there are fifty thousand souls.

Soccer is their religion
And any religion denies atheism.

I am the football fan vicar,
This is where my congregation
  stands.
Listen to their hymns of praise
And hymns of glory.
This is where the sermon must
  take place.
Not in an empty church
With an empty story.

CHORUS:
(Sing)
Vincent Vincent, Vincent Vincent
Vincent Vincent, Vincent Vincent,
Vincent Vincent,
He is the greatest in the land,
All praise our Vincent,
All praise him,
All praise our Vincent,
All praise him.
And he shall play for ever and
  ever,
For ever and ever, for ever, ever,
  ever,
Our Vincent, our Vincent,
Our Vincent Vincent Vincent.
CITY'S KING,
Our Vincent, our Vincent,
CITY'S KING,
Our Vincent, our Vincent,

He is the greatest in the land,
And he shall play for ever and
  ever,
Our Vincent, our Vincent,
Our Vincent Vincent Vincent,
VINCENT VINCENT.

(*Enter* HARRY)

VICAR : Well, lad, I see you're a
  City fan.

(HARRY *takes his scarf off.*)

No need to take it off, lad, not in
the house of God. I'm sure God
has a little bit of favour for his own
team.

HARRY : I just dropped in, like.

VICAR : Got something on your
mind ? Want any help, do you ?

HARRY : Help ? No. I'm looking
around.

VICAR : Oh yes, do, go on. Don't
let me stop you.

HARRY : Do you have to pray and
that ?

VICAR : Not unless you feel the
need, son ?

HARRY : No.

VICAR : It's not necessary. The
Lord sees into your heart, you
know. He can judge what you're
feeling. Same as from the terraces
you can judge the feeling of your
centre half by his actions.

HARRY : We were never church-
goers in our house. But my sister
watches the hymn singing on the
telly.

VICAR : Ah, there's some rare old
tunes, aren't there ? Have you
heard them singing 'Rock of
Ages' at Wembley ?

HARRY : But they change the
words. They change the words.

VICAR : But it's still God's tune,
you see. And he knows. The song
goes up to him all the same.

HARRY : There sometimes seems
nothing to live for, you know.
Nothing. Jobs, nor life, nor nothing.

VICAR : What ? And us fifth in the
League ? You're kidding. Nothing
to live for ? We just have to pick
up points from Liverpool and
Leeds and we're there. The
mission to the north has got to
bring down the walls of Goodison
Park.

HARRY : Yes. But like, it doesn't
seem worth settling down. There
is nothing to serve.

VICAR : They also serve who only
stand and wait. Why, it's like a
football match, religion is ; it
would be nothing without the
terraces full of spectators. God
battles with the Devil in front of a
full gate. Crush barriers up in the
greatest stadium of all.

HARRY : But is there any purpose
in life, see ?

VICAR : Purpose ? When Saturday comes you find a purpose.
You go out there and sing to the
glory of your team. Well, God is
that team. They are God made
creatures, in his image, those
lads are ; and your songs of glory
go to him.

HARRY : But there's no faith, no
nothing, your church is empty. I
don't want to go, nobody does.
But you've got to have faith in
life, to believe something.

VICAR : Believe that God has
transferred his house to the football pitch, that's what to believe.
Look for his sermon and his lesson
in your team, look at the clash of
faiths between the infidels of

Wolverhampton and us. You'll get God's message, it's everywhere.

HARRY: Why, you stupid little berk; no wonder your church is empty. You're trying to be smart wi' the football, trying to get in with us. If God was real, he would have us in here. Football . . . *is nothing.*

VICAR: There are some you can't get by any methods, you see. (*He goes*)

HARRY:
Is there no faith in life but football?
Is there no path to heaven but League Division One?
No Judgement Day but Wembley for the Cup Final?
A team is an empty thing, I see it now,
You support them in all weathers,
Wear their rosettes,
Red and white scarves, hats,
The City plumage, the City feathers.
They give you faith in life,
They have a series of quick wins and gain the top of the table,
You worship them if they're on form.

They're your gods,
You would die for them
If you were able.
But one day they'll let you down.
They aren't Christ Almighty.
They'll hit a bad patch,
Go tumbling down
One season. You wait and see,
They'll go tumbling down the League:
Relegation, Division Two, or Three,
Then you'll see it from another view
The football terrace is the fool's pew.

CHORUS:
(*Sing*)
Bring us that Cup
Of burning gold,
Bring us that trophy we desire,
Bring us it back
O team of old,
Come back the champions or retire.
We shall not cease to spur you on
Nor shall our rattles fail to sound
Till we have brought the FA Cup
To City's noble sacred ground.

From *Zigger-Zagger*, 1970

ANDY CAPP

I'VE BEEN DROPPED FROM THE FOOTBALL TEAM, FLO! HUH! COULDN'T TELL ME TO MY FACE~!

THE CAPTAIN SAYS I'M GETTIN' INDECISIVE IN FRONT OF GOAL!

ME? INDECISIVE? NEVER!!

D'YER THINK I SHOULD ANSWER IT, OR IGNORE IT, OR STUFF IT DOWN 'IS THROAT, OR WHAT? NOW LET'S CONSIDER....

18

Burnley v. Newcastle United

Julie Welch

Newcastle bludgeoned their way into this semi-final with perspiration and choler in equal measure, and even if yesterday's savage labours at Hillsborough had not been partnered by skill, no one would deny that they were a suitable case for Wembley.

Powerful and self-convinced, their urge for victory was almost carnivorous, and poor Burnley, no slouches themselves when it came to effort, were well and truly digested at the end.

Recipients of everyone's backpats and ribands will, of course, be Macdonald, whose early blustering around the goalmouth metamorphosed into something far more deadly.

But if the gratitude is to be fairly apportioned, it was the marvellous Hibbitt and the trailing McDermott who between them turned this match from a rather scruffy affair to the second-half landslide which Burnley suddenly had on their hands.

All the early frenzy belonged to the Newcastle supporters, massed in black and white profusion on the high terraces like some dirty,

vast and fleshy snowdrift, against whose self-righteous bellowings the noise of the Burnley crowd was reduced to a modest peep. On the pitch, things were not so one-sided.

When small Nulty rose gigantically to head the ball against the crossbar, when Tudor turned in a ball from MacDonald only to see it blasted hugely over the bar, the pattern of missed chances seemed to be set.

Certainly, in neatness and imagination, Newcastle were being outplayed, the ball sifting and glancing with disturbing speed through the Burnley midfield. But up front Fletcher was a toiling disappointment and Casper spent much of his time yoked firmly between Howard and Moncur.

Dobson tried his level-headed best, just missing out on the half-hour with his scuttling, ducking header; the ensuing commotion ended with MacDonald belting up the left wing and delivering a shot which razored past the far post while the Burnley defence hurtled gamely after it.

Generally, though, it was a

"It'll be an hour before we reach the ground in this traffic. Anyone else desperate?"

rather soused and flat first half, ending with Hibbitt in a low sorry heap after a foul by Noble; and when the second half began in like manner, the pointers were more toward villainy than a victory for anyone.

Noble, this captive tank of Burnley's, had motored down the right wing and, squashing Smith, no player to be monkeyed about with, received a booking for his misbehaviour. Smith avenged himself with a churlish little foul on Nulty, who had done no one harm, and perhaps it was best for the quality of the game that, after due Newcastle pressure, Mac-Donald did his duty at last.

Fouled, inevitably by Noble, as he homed magnificently on goal, MacDonald faltered, and weighed up his chances of a penalty before deciding to thresh on. Stevenson blanked out his first shot with great bravura; MacDonald merely careered to the right, and though Waldron poked his torso at him from the goalline, the ball whistled smartly past the unfortunate No 5's ear. MacDonald was chased back to the circle by an exalting Tudor as the New-castle supporters orchestrated their joy.

Burnley took a while to collapse, but they were surely undermined, giving away two successive corners in which only Newcastle's over-eagerness and MacDonald's slapdash misheader saved them from immediate disaster. True, they were still functioning up front, McFaul producing two prodigious saves from Collins and James: one abdomen-crippling catch and one urgent lambast over the bar.

After a wasted Burnley free kick near the Newcastle penalty area, Hibbitt salvaged the ball, spotted that MacDonald was rocketing on his right and passed to him. Thompson could offer no defence nor could Stevenson, who merely had the displeasure of watching the pesky, bulky centre-forward clout the ball unanswerably past him.

As the frothing, hawking, roaring noise of the Newcastle supporters rose into the Sheffield air, McFaul produced a save the way conjurors produce pigeons, jabbing out his left hand at a point-blank Casper volley to send the ball floating magically over the crossbar. It was Burnley's last chance—perhaps their only real chance—and they could not take it.

'Some of my players cried, and I cried with them,' said Burnley manager Jimmy Adamson mournfully afterwards. 'If only we could have got a goal in the first half. . . . But when you have a centre-forward like MacDonald, you can have 10 bad players and might still win.'

By then on a tide of Ey-ay-addios and seat cushions, the Newcastle supporters had over-boiled into a victory they had always claimed was their team's by right. With the mileage of those two replayed quarter-finals behind them, with everybody condoning their presence at Sheffield yesterday, and with Malcolm MacDonald claiming he is good enough for the England team, Newcastle made it deservedly. As Joe Harvey said : 'It all came right in the end.'

BURNLEY : Stevenson : Noble, Newton, Dobson, Waldron, Thomson, Nulty, Casper, Fletcher, Collins, James, Sub : Hankin

NEWCASTLE UNITED : McFaul : Craig, Clark, McDermott, Howard, Moncur, Cassidy, Smith, MacDonald, Tudor, Hibbitt, Sub : Kennedy.

Referee : G. Hill (Leicester)

From *The Observer*, 1974

FOCUS ON FACT—*The Football Story (19)*   By Gary Keane & Neville Randall

1880s. FOOTBALLERS BEGAN THE DECADE IN **KNICKERBOCKERS**. CHANGED TO **CUTS** – TIGHT TROUSERS CUT AT FIRST BELOW THE KNEES, THEN ON AND ABOVE IT. CHANGING INTO **SHORTS**.

1891. **UMPIRES** OFF THE FIELD WERE REPLACED BY A **REFEREE** ON IT, WITH WHISTLE AND NOTEBOOK. EMPOWERED TO GIVE DECISIONS WITHOUT WAITING FOR APPEALS, AND AWARD PENALTIES FOR GOAL AREA FOULS.

1886. LONDON. A NEW CLUB WAS FORMED. ROYAL ARSENAL. OFFERING JOBS FOR PLAYERS AS ARSENAL WORKERS.

1894. A SOUTHERN LEAGUE. EARLY MEMBERS : SOUTHAMPTON, TOTTENHAM, BRISTOL CITY AND CHELSEA. BECOMING THIRD DIVISION SOUTH IN 1920.

19

Greenberg

Brian Glanville

Loyal and skeletal, Greenberg appeared one day in the United press-box, the latest of Freeman's friends. These were the early fifties, when there was still residual hope that Freeman would one day be rich, be famous, be all the things he'd promised to be, and knew he should be.

Kind and cocksure, with his puns, his spectacles, his trilby hat—but over forty, now—he covered games for the *Dispatch*, and brought his friends, who had no right to be there. Of these, Greenberg, though so silent, was the most noticeable yet. He was very tall, unfailingly intense, given to long, fawn, shapeless raincoats, which he wore like shrouds; to a brown, high-crowned hat, worn without fantasy, flush on the crown of his head, where Freeman's trilby swooped like a kestrel. He never smiled. His eyes, small and myopic, behind tortoiseshell spectacles, were brown; the eyes of a sad, old dog.

When Freeman talked, he listened, as if listening were an active function. The tension of his thin body, the very inclination of his head, proclaimed: I'm listening, look at me, and *you* should listen, too. Later, as he gradually relaxed, he went one further, took to nodding; later still, to murmured choruses: 'Joe's right, you know.'

One saw him only at the two North London grounds, United and Rovers; perhaps because Freeman's writ ran no further, perhaps because he himself had a sense of the appropriate. For he was all North London, its quintessence, the distillation of its fogs, its ugly streets and shopping arcades, its multiple stores, its drab semi-detacheds. It was impossible to picture him in the country, unless it were in the middle of some field; a straggling urban sparrow. God knows what he did for a living; one imagined him travelling in ladies' garments, dealing in ugly furniture, doing something honest and dim, modestly rewarding, without prospects.

'Him?' said Freeman, oblivious throughout of the signs of growing independence, the first, faint, rumblings of self-determination, 'Stoke Newington, I think he lives. Or Stamford Hill.' It was as if he, too, granted Greenberg no existence beyond the press-box, no ambitions that were not discipular. 'Joe's right. If they'd listened to Joe . . . Joe *knows* the game.'

Quixote and Pancha, I thought, watching them one day from behind as they moved across the grey waste of the United car park, Greenberg adapting his long gaunt strides to match the shorter, chirpier gait of Freeman, as he loomed above him. Yet which, on second thoughts, was Quixote, which Sancho Panza? Freeman, certainly, would have no doubts; he saw himself as a crusader. 'The top soccer controversialist of our day,' he had called himself, in the publicity hand-out for his latest enterprise, 'Football Programmes International'.

'Wonderful,' said Greenberg who, in his second press-box season, had more to say. 'A wonderful idea of Joe's. A man in Rio wants to collect Arsenal programmes, so now he can do it.'

But the scheme, like all Freeman's schemes, had collapsed; other countries, for the most part, didn't issue programmes. 'But if they *had*!' cried Greenberg. 'What a wonderful idea!'

Our conversations, those we had, took place in the car park, or in the tiny, crowded press-rooms at Rovers and United, over saucerless white cups of thick, undrinkable tea, over cheese and spam sandwiches, over the occasional prize of a small cake. Around us, other journalists shoved and bustled in their lemming rush towards the tea-urn. Elbows challenged one's cup of tea, feet ground into one's toes; Greenberg towered above the ruck like an ostrich, his Adam's apple bobbing with emotion. 'Ronnie Klein,' he'd say, naming an editor who once published Freeman in his short-lived magazine. 'It went to his head. Ten-guinea shirts. Fifty guinea suits. And telling *Joe* what to do! *Joe!*'

Slowly, then, he was taking on a life of his own, though one noticed it only in retrospect. To talk at all was the first step, the next, to talk when Freeman was not beside him, like a puppeteer, even if Freeman was still almost his only subject.

The time came, though, when Freeman was not; instead the subject was his nephews. Both were doing very well, and one guessed he couldn't be married, had perennially resigned himself to the status of admiring uncle. One nephew was a brilliant boy, 17—'he's going to sit a scholarship to Cambridge.' The other was younger, 14—'not a student, he'll never make a student, but a natural footballer. I watch all his school games, Saturday mornings, before I come on here. This morning; what a goal! Left-footed! I only wish you'd been there to see it!'

Faithful and opaque, Freeman took him for granted. Freeman noticed nothing, continuing to make puns, cheerfully lay down the law, deplore his bad luck in the past: 'And it was all fixed! The job was mine!' Greenberg, like the rest, had his function—that of Chorus—in return for which he saw the match for nothing. But Greenberg wasn't like the rest. ·

Next season, his third in the press-boxes, one suddenly became aware he had cut adrift. There he was, one autumn afternoon at Rovers, high up in the back row, sitting by himself; or rather, sitting between two reporters, neither of whom was Freeman. The same hat perched incongruously on his head, he blinked out over the field through the same spectacles. Baffled, I looked round for Freeman and at last saw him, rows and rows away, far down across the gangway; itself a frontier. Had they quarrelled, I wondered? Had Panza seen through Quixote, Quixote been disappointed in Panza? But in that case, why was Greenberg still there? Over the years, Choruses had come, been used, and had departed; interchangeable, replaceable.

At half-time in the press-room, where the steam of tea mingled with the steam of soaking raincoats, they did not speak to one another. In the cases of Greenberg, gaunt and opaque, it might have meant anything or nothing, but there was something to the set of Freeman's back, turned consistently to Greenberg, which implied a huffy consciousness he was there.

It seemed to me, as the weeks went by and Greenberg changed with them, that Freeman increasingly took on the baffled aspect of a Frankenstein deserted by his monster.

In his next stage, Greenberg grew strangely interested in minutiae. It was guilt, perhaps, a lurking awareness that however long he haunted press-boxes, he had no right to be there. This, though he was always kind and patient with young journalists, sombrely welcoming, helping them decide just who had hit the post, which had kicked off the line.

So, in this new phase, he came to care about attendance figures, about those little scraps of pasteboard passed along each row of journalists after half-time, bearing the number of spectators. 'Did you get it?' he would ask, turning his anxious, sad, cadaverous face to the row behind him. 'Forty-five thousand and what? Three-three-two. Thank you.' And, relieved, he would write it down very carefully in his programme.

Then there were the goalscorers, or rather, not so much the goalscorers as the goal *makers*, pursued with almost genealogical zeal. 'Who gave him the ball?' the hollowed face would turn to ask.

'Lewis.'

'No, not him. The pass *before* that.'

I never saw him with his hat off, nor his mackintosh, even when spring came and the brighter days, when the shun shone on the United car park, on as a desert, gleamed—if you walked down the hill—from the glassy sides of Rovers' towering stands. If he did take the hat off he'd be bald, I knew; would have to be bald, his skull a vast egg, crossed by a few adventurous strands. One almost felt he had been born bald, been born wearing the hat, although beneath the brim of it, hair grew in bushy irrelevance down the back of his neck.

'My nephew,' he said, one day at Rovers, when I met him walking up the wretched street from the Tube. 'The brilliant one . . .?' I began, then changed it to the Cambridge one?'

'No, no,' he said, 'that's not till Christmas, not the scholarship. The other one.'

'The footballer?'

'That's right. I've talked to Johnny Wilkinson.' This was the United manager, a silent man with a thick red neck who sat, anguished, in the back row of the directors' box, suffering each mistake, identifying with each kick. From the press-box, right behind him, one could almost tell the state of a game, simply by looking at his neck.

'That's good,' I said.

'He's interested. He'll send a scout.'

'That's marvellous.'

Often, now, he would be in the press-box when Freeman wasn't, suggesting total independence, access to passes of his own. And he grew more and more assertive, no longer craning on the edge of groups like an apologetic giraffe. Nor did he merely participate; he would contradict, interrupt, quite impervious; spluttering his disagreement, intruding in a sudden welter of words. 'Yes, but that's not the point . . . it isn't . . . I mean, a man like that, a centre-forward, he's *entitled* to score goals.'

Now *he* was Quixote, tilting at shibbeloths, at self-styled lions of Fleet Street. 'What about Dimmock?' he once cried, when a group of us one day were listen-to a monologue, by a lion, on the failings of managers. The lion turned, ready to devour him, then said nothing. Greenberg, all bone and gristle, could plainly never be devoured. 'A man like Dimmock,' he said, his cavernous face drawn tighter than ever by the violence of his sincerity. 'Where do you ever see an outside-left like him? I was a boy. My father took me.'

In the New Year, he said to me, 'My nephew. You remind me of him,' and I said, confused, 'The one who may turn pro?'

'No, no,' he said, 'the brilliant one. The Cambridge one. He's going there. He got his scholarship.'

'That's wonderful,' I said.

'In Science,' he said. '*Natural* Science. His headmaster at the school said they've never had a boy like that. Believe me, he'll end up as one of those . . . those nuclear . . .'

'Physicists,' I heard myself say.

'That or the other thing. The rockets.'

'You must be very proud of him.'

'I am,' he said, 'I am,' and I

remembered how he'd once been proud of Freeman.

Freeman never spoke to him, nor of him, and intrigued as I was, I could not bring myself to mention him to Freeman, greyer and less jaunty with the years, his jokes feebler, his ambitions no longer advertised. Once only in conversation did I mention Freeman's name to Greenberg, half experimentally. 'Spoiled himself,' said Greenberg, in a perfunctory mutter. 'He spoiled himself, Joe.' It sounded like an obituary.

Next August, when the evening games began, Greenberg brought his nephew, the Cambridge one, brought him into the press-box: 'My nephew; he's going to Cambridge.' The nephew was quite a good-looking boy, with a soft, full face, and wavy black hair; tall, though not as tall as Greenberg. He was modest, polite, and he seemed unembarrassed; perhaps, over the years of promise and fulfilment, he had grown used to his uncle's fulsomeness.

'You two,' said Greenberg, introducing us. 'You'd have a lot in common.' I thought, wrongly and wonderingly, that the wheel had come full circle; Greenberg, an interloper in the press-box, was now bringing guests of his own.

But I was wrong. One windy afternoon at United, squeezed between a parked Bentley and a parked Jaguar, I saw him in tense conversation with one of United's directors; though all Greenberg's conversations were tense. The director, like every United direct-or, had about him the prosaic, suspicious air of a successful grocer, uneasy beyond the safety of his counter. He looked up at the gaunt, wobbling, talking head on its long, thin neck with a wondering wariness of which Greenberg seemed quite unconscious. They—or Greenberg—were talking, I supposed, of the other nephew, the footballer, of whom one still heard from time to time; he was having a trial with Finchley, the amateurs; he was 'going to sign forms' for United, amateur forms; 'his father wants him in the business.'

Six weeks later, when next I covered a United game, Greenberg was in the directors' box. At first I could not believe it, was sure I had mistaken the front row of the press-box for the back row of the directors' box. But I hadn't. The narrow, bony, raincoated shoulders, the irrelevant fringe of hair beneath the hat, sat, indeed, in the back row of the directors' box, five places down from Johnny Wilkinson, the manager.

Looking round for someone to discuss it with, I saw, in a corner of the press-box, Freeman; he, in turn, looking at the hat, the scraggy neck, with a thin, wounded smile.

During the match, I noticed that Greenberg's behaviour in the directors' box did not vary; he still, when a goal was scored, spoke anxiously to those around him, making notes on his programme, though he did not speak to the journalists behind him. At half-time, in the tea-room, Freeman's eyes met mine. *'Chuzpah,'* he said. 'You know what *chuzpah* means? The Jewish boy who shot his father and mother and then said don't hang me, I'm an orphan.'

I nodded, though I saw it differently. *Chuzpah* meant cheek and bounce, effrontery, and where was Greenberg's?

A month later, I saw him in the directors' box again, his nephew —the brilliant one—was beside him. Now, when we met, he was still cordial in his taut, unrelated way, but there were modulations; a hint that he was privy to secrets. There were times, when he talked about United, that he said 'we'. 'If we get a couple of quick goals . . . that was never a goal, that one; they robbed us.' The club, it almost seemed, had taken the place once filled by Freeman: 'the best in England, greatest players, greatest manager. You know our trouble? We play too *much* football.'

January, with its fog and cup-ties, its sheets of grey, heavy rain assailing the bleak stadium, gave way to February, to March, to spring, the Cup Final, and the terminal evening games; the pitches brown and grassless, mud flats with a fringe of green. Then it was summer, and hiatus; foreign tours, transfers, practice matches; a process as regular as the seasons themselves.

United opened the new championship with a home match, which I went to report. Inside the car park, Freeman met me. *'Ha*-llo, Brian. Heard the one about the two Jewish hairdressers?' I listened, tried to laugh, then I saw Greenberg, getting out of a Daimler, the vice-chairman's Daimler, still awkward as an ostrich. Rain-coated as always, he stood for a moment in the sunshine, there in the middle of the car park, peering dimly round. Yet there was something in the stance of the absurd, thin body, something in the poise of the head on its meagre neck, which suggested he was not looking for people, but rather looking round a new domain.

It was only when his gaze reached Freeman that it paused, then fell and, clumsily, he turned away.

'Didn't you know?' asked Freeman, as we watched the tall, stooped figure moving with the vice-chairman towards the officials' entrance. His right hand held a programme out to me, thumb agitating on the front cover, and there, beneath the pyramid of the directors' names, I saw the new one: L.B. Greenberg.

From *The Thing He Loves,* 1973

85

20

Christmas With Regnar

John Arlott

The idea of Christmas Day with no football would have been unthinkable to 'Regnar'; unless it fell on Sunday, of course. Under the *nom-de-plume* he invented for himself, 'Regnar' reported Rangers' football matches for the local paper between the two wars.

Now the old man is as dead as the kind of football he wrote about, and the way he wrote about it. He never saw spectators run on to the field except, rarely, to cheer the winning of promotion. Otherwise, they snarled, booed and cheered; but, apart from a few grounds—one in London and one in Yorkshire were well known for it—strife was rare; and even there a few police could suppress it in moments. 'Regnar' considered boy spectators—even the un-armed species of his day—as irritants: they disturbed his literary processes. They regarded him with some respect, the players with awe; an autograph was a privilege, not a right.

'Regnar' had virtually no contact with the players; he con-trived no 'angles'—would have been horrified at the thought of probing beneath the surface—and 'revealed' nothing. The foot-ballers themselves were generally competitive yet, uncontradictor-ily, self-sufficient men. They were grateful to be free from the pit, mill or workshop, earning the Third Division average of £6 or perhaps £6 10s a week. In 1922 the League fixed the maximum wage at £8 during the playing season and £7 for the remaining fifteen weeks; few outside the First Division were paid the top rate, which was not increased until 1945.

The reporter's effective link with the club was through the man-ager who, from time to time, handed him such information as he saw fit for publication. 'Reg-nar' might mildly ask—but never demand—more, nor sought it elsewhere. Sometimes the club would give a party after the Christmas match when the play-ers were served with a beer and 'Regnar' forsook his normal ale to take a status-symbol whisky with the directors.

'Regnar's' identification with Rangers was complete. When they scored there was an air of divine right about the act. A goal to their opponents was malign fate or act of God. It was fitting—indeed, their true destiny—that they should win. When they lost he grieved at the injustice, sought excuses rather than reasons. So far as could be inferred from his reports or conversations, goals were not planned or created but occurred by some process of Olympian decision. Certainly they seemed always to impinge on him as isolated and somewhat mysterious events.

At some point of his career he presumably—though not certainly—recognized that the events which take place on a football field are limited in extent and language and, as a result, he became, if not a master, at least an aspiring student, of the synonym. On his great days he could avoid using the precise word for anything throughout the duration of a report. He was a man of his time: he never in his life referred to a match as a 'clash'; and only rarely as a match; it was a 'derby', 'duel', 'contest', 'tourney', 'battle', 're-newal of hostilities', 'struggle', ('epic' or, at best, 'titanic'). It was almost unknown for one of his players to shoot or head a goal. They 'drove home', 'converted', 'nodded', 'equalized', 'netted', 'notched', 'reduced the leeway', 'increased their advantage', 'applied the finishing touch' or 'left the custodian helpless'.

He had a special set of phrases for Christmas Day matches. Occasionally he would note that 'the holiday spirit was in evidence' or, in a more extreme circumstance, that 'a few spectators, alas, had celebrated not too wisely, but too well'; 'The opposing leader set the sphere a-rolling (it was simply rolling in non-holiday matches) in a seasonable snowstorm'.

If the referee seemed to him too harsh on Rangers 'The arbiter showed little seasonal goodwill towards the homesters': if he gave a penalty to the other side 'the official proved a veritable Father Christmas to the visitors'. The scorer of a goal—in a day before footballers (or most other working men) aspired to turkey—had 'earned his slice of chicken' or 'entitled himself to that Christmas pudding and mincepies'.

His attitude towards foul play—if he ever saw it—was peculiarly

"I know it's very nice, Doris, but reserve team football isn't going to get him the England Cap he promised me."

naïve. One Rangers back—the amiably loose-lipped, ponderously built, thug, Percy—if tormented by a ball-player would, from time to time in his frustration, aim at him a kick which could well have amputated the lower part of his legs : but Regnar could never bring himself to describe Percy as anything more than 'robust'. On Christmas Day, however, he might go so far as to comment that 'the traditional Yuletide goodwill towards men was not always in evidence.'

Above all, if his team won he could open his report with 'Rangers brought bubbling Christmas cheer to their adherents with a resounding trumph over their old adversaries . . .' He could close it with 'these two precious points made a most acceptable Christmas Box for Rangers' or even 'This victory filled the blue-and-whites' cup of Christmas cheer to overflowing'.

From *The Guardian*

"Give the ref a chance, lads! Back ten yards ...!"

21

The Very Last Word

Ian Wooldridge

The fourth attempt to kidnap Brian Clough—ostensibly even more boring than the other three —conceals an unbelievable story of international intrigue.

While other reporters mingled with weeping families at the forbidding gates of Brighton and Hove football ground, Sportsmail's chief investigative actionreplay analyst Jim Molecule was achieving another of his worldwide scoops.

Today I became the first British reporter to parachute into the picture-postcard Mediterranean package-deal holiday isle of Majorca disguised as an unemployed flamenco dancer.

Brian Clough greeted me with his customary warmth. 'Get out,' he cried. He was wearing a Fidel Castro flak-jacket and straining to pick up the crackling news bulletins from rebel Radio Littlehampton.

'They've just reported I'm dead,' he said. 'Do they not yet understand that I'm immortal? I slipped out of the Goldstone ground by a secret door in the groundsman's shed. To avoid attention I was

wearing the robes of a Greek orthodox archbishop. Mind you, that's all off the record.'

I produced a magnum of his favourite Veuve Cliquot '69. 'I am chief investigative action-replay analyst of a great newspaper,' I said, 'and I have come here to probe the labyrinths of your mind. Are you going to Leeds or not?'

Clough drank deeply. His voice lowered an octave, emerging now as only a medium-high-pitch shriek. 'You don't understand, do you?' he said. 'You don't understand a bloody thing.'

'That is why I am here,' I replied evenly, 'to find out.'

Clough drained his glass. 'I should have thought a chief investigative analyst would have had more brain,' he said. 'Don't you understand that it's sixteen days since I appeared on the telly and *nearly five weeks* since I made banner headlines in all the newspapers.

'Hombre, a man can be forgotten in that time. Particularly when the England cricket team are winning three Tests in a row and the British Lions are rampaging through South Africa not that they should have gone there in the first place.'

'Are you suggesting,' I ventured, 'that you enjoy being the centre of attraction? That publicity to you is what fillet steak is to the rest of us?'

Clough consulted his English-Spanish dictionary, searching for a devastating riposte. 'Nada,' he said eventually, which is Spanish for 'Good morning.'

Around us the mules fidgeted. The interview was not going well. Clough reached for a copy of *Death in the Afternoon* and began searching for the pictures. He was tired of the conversation.

'We have been all through this before,' I said. 'First it was Derby County fans trying to get you back. Nothing came of that. Then it was the Shah of Persia luring you with jewels and Mercedes and a couple of oil wells. Nothing came of that. Then it was Aston Villa offering a queen's ransom and unlimited expenses. Nothing came of that either.

'Now, after unfulfilled threats to go into politics and unrequited offers to take over the English soccer managership, you are apparently in line for the Leeds job.

'It occurs to me that so many thousands of tons of newsprint have been devoted to your non-activities that there is extreme danger of my five million readers becoming bored with your very name.'

A flicker of concern rippled Clough's brow.

'Jim, lad,' he said, 'it's just that you don't understand the pressure that those of us in the public eye have to live with. Only men like Kissinger and myself can understand that, men who hold the destinies of millions in the palms of their hands.'

He sighed, thinking hard. 'What about if we say that what I told you about my escape in archbishop's robes *wasn't* off the record? Would you like to write about it?'

'No,' I said, 'this time, once and for all, I want to know if your intentions are honourable. Do you intend to go to Leeds or don't you? Do you intend to go anywhere? Or are you just stringing us all along again to keep your name in the public eye?'

Brian Clough, professor emeritus of the calculated indiscretion, past-master of the provocative phrase, looked alarmed.

'Okay,' he said, 'I'll come clean. I've got a hell of a problem. I've just been offered the managership of the Springbok Rugger team and the conductorship of the Berlin Philharmonic. Do you think you can find something to write about now?'

He pointed to a telephone and indicated generously that I needn't reverse the charges.

From the *Daily Mail*, 1974

22

Leeds United v. Ujpest Dozsa

Geoffrey Green

Leeds United pulled down the curtain on Ujpest Dozsa, leaders of the Hungarian League, at Elland Road last night. Building on their 2-1 lead in Budapest of a fortnight ago, they reached the quarter-final round of the European Cup, and with Feyenoord out already, the big names now left are Barcelona, led by Johan Cruyff, and the West Germans, Bayern Munich, who hold the trophy.

Leeds are now halfway through the long haul and must wait until January before they know their next opponents in the draw. Goals by McQueen at the half-hour and then two more by Bremner and Yorath in the first 20 minutes of the second-half saw the Hungarians held in chancery. It seemed that Leeds, once they had scored, could flush the game whenever they wanted and they did so.

Following the two men sent off in Budapest and the others booked on that occasion, this proved to be a carefully polite match. All through it, one watched the reactions of Bremner, now playing only his second senior match since the start of the season. Clearly, he had sat by for weeks with a savage patience. But now, leading his team with authority, there was a quiet involvement as he played his way back into things. By the end, there was the sight of a new young man, the 17-year-old Welsh youth international, Harris, who was substituted for Yorath with 20 minutes to go so that he could get a feel of the big time. Clearly, this young player has a future. He was found by the scout who once discovered the great John Charles, and on that eye, I think any of us can rely.

Leeds won as they liked. Ujpest Dozsa had a sensitive technique with players like Fazekas and Toth clever in midfield. But the great Bene of old was a shadow and the Hungarian build-up provided the slow, deliberate movements of some night watchman. Nor was there any of that hungry finish that once one knew. Against this, men like the long-striding Madeley, McQueen and Hunter—until he hobbled off with a knee injury before half-time—were the masters with Giles and Bremner also setting up attack after attack as Cooper time after time over-lapped down the left flank.

If only Clarke this night had been in touch, Leeds could have doubled their score. But the ball constantly kept running unkindly for him. Or was it merely that his timing was out? On this form, certainly, he will find no place in the England side against Portugal this month in the European championship.

With the Leeds defence as tight as a vault, it was only a question of time for their opening goal. With a quarter of an hour left to the interval it arrived at last after a series of near misses by the unhappy Clarke. As in Budapest, it was a combination of a free-kick by Giles—this time from left to right, after Cooper had been fouled—that saw the lanky McQueen rise above the crowd to put Leeds ahead with an aggregate advantage of 3-1. A minute after the interval, a flying save by Szigeti from Cooper saw a corner forced on the right. Here some short passing between Lorimer and Giles saw Yorath head Lorimer's final centre against the crossbar. But there was the hungry Bremner to loop his header home over the goalkeeper as he fell backwards off balance.

After that Leeds took things quietly in their stride, no doubt keeping themselves away from injury with their League position at home yet to be repaired. Finally, with 25 minutes to go, as a superlative move involving Cooper, Reaney, Yorath, Clarke, Bremner and Madeley saw Clarke finally nod Madeley's centre square for Yorath to head home number three. That was it. It was a criss-cross pattern which left the Hungarians cross-eyed.

LEEDS UNITED: D. Harvey, P. Reaney, G. McQueen, N. Hunter (sub. T. Cherry) T. Cooper, W. Bremner, P. Madeley, J. Giles, P. Lorimer, A. Clarke, T. Yorath (sub. C. Harris)
UJPEST DOZSA: K. Szigeti, E. Kolar, E. Dunai, A. Sarlos, J. Keliner, A. Toth, L. Fazekas, S. Zambo, L. Fekete (sub. A. Dunai) F. Bene, L. Nagy (sub. A. Torocsik)
Referee: A. Delcourt (Belgium)

From *The Times*, 1974

FOCUS ON FACT—*The Football Story (20)*   **By Gary Keane & Neville Randall**

1884. BRITISH SOLDIERS ON SHORE LEAVE PLAYED FOOTBALL IN BRAZIL. IN 1901 OSCAR COX, BRITISH RESIDENT, FOUNDED THE FLUMINENSE FOOTBALL CLUB IN RIO. BRAZILIANS TOOK UP THE GAME WITH ZEST.

1892. ITALY. DR. JAMES SPENSLEY AND OTHER RESIDENT BRITISH FOUNDED THE GENOA CRICKET AND FOOTBALL CLUB. BY THE END OF THE CENTURY BRITONS HAD SPREAD FOOTBALL ROUND THE WORLD.

SPENSLEY

1904. PARIS. SIX COUNTRIES FORMED AN INTERNATIONAL FEDERATION OF ASSOCIATION FOOTBALL. FIFA.

1908. LONDON. FIFA STAGED THE FIRST FOOTBALL TOURNAMENT, AT THE OLYMPIC GAMES, WON BY THE UNITED KINGDOM. FIRST CHAMPIONS OF THE WORLD.

23

Many Happier Returns

Hugh McIlvanney

Images of the 1974 World Cup, blurred as they were by rain and the work-grimed landscape of the Ruhr, will not linger in the mind as brightly as those of the sunny festival in Mexico four years earlier. Exoticism alone might have given the competition of 1970 a considerable advantage but in the end it provided much more practical reasons for setting it above the one that has just finished.

Leaving aside the irony that when it came to achieving an overall sense of effective organisation it was the Latin rather than the Teutonic approach that impressed, the Mexico World Cup was distinguished by a coherent progress towards climax on the field. Brazil advanced with growing conviction on that championship, letting the rhythms of their football swell steadily until these made an engulfing—though thoughtfully orchestrated—clamour by the time poor Italy were offered as victims in the final.

By this summer the deep inhibitions of Mario Zagalo (those shadowy apprehensions that gather on the edge of his nature and make him such a devotee of spiritualism, such a prey to superstition) were manifesting themselves in the graceless negativism of his team. In West Germany the Brazilians, with several striking exceptions, most memorably Luis Pereira, played like desperate men on the rug from their own ordinariness.

Holland took up the banner of adventurous football and for most of the way they carried it with a glorious flourish. Even with their acknowledged weaknesses in defence, they were, without question, the finest team in the competition. At their best they attacked with such speed, variety, imagination and verve that Muhammed Ali might just have permitted an analogy with himself. Yet there was always the suspicion that anti-climax would be their reward and so it proved in the final.

My own feeling is that the goal they took in less than a minute, when the great Cruyff's electrifying run from the sweeper's position alarmed the the Germans

into conceding an unchallenge-
able penalty, was ultimately their
undoing. It persuaded them to
attempt a careful, even-paced
game throughout the first half
instead of seeking to build the
momentum on which all their
previous successes had been
based.

They did revert to character
after the interval but ill-luck
barred their way and the Cup was
won by a West German side that
had many virtues but little of the
devouring brilliance that made
Helmut Schoen's men, with
Netzer's inspiration, the European champions in 1972.

Poland, surely the happiest and
most deserving collectors of third
prize in the history of the event,
and gallant, entertaining Sweden
are among the others we will
remember vividly.

Of course no Scot can be expected to overlook the fact that
his nation emerged as the only
one of the 16 competitors to remain unbeaten, but even those of
us who brim with admiration for
the magnificent job done by the
players who so frightened Brazil
and Yugoslavia must wince at
some of the more extravagant
interpretations of what was
accomplished.

For a start, it is somewhat easier
to stay unbeaten if you leave for
home after three first-class
matches than it is if you have to
play a total of seven, including
the final, as Holland did. So only
if the tongue is in the cheek is it
permissible to dwell on that particular distinction.

Similarly, the welcome the
Scots party received at Glasgow
Airport from 10,000 of their
countrymen grateful for having
had their pride nourished in a
World Cup after years of humi-
liating failure was an utterly and
rather moving gesture. Even naming at least one street in Scotland
after Willie Ormond is acceptable
enough, but when people start
talking about a celebration dinner
at Edinburgh Castle we are bound
to wonder how such a flood of
euphoria could be released by
such a partial success.

A reminder of how partial it was
came from a friend whose intense
Scottishness is balanced by an
inclination to remain within
shouting distance of reality when
discussing his own race. 'Alright,
we were unbeaten in a World
Cup and that's marvellous,' he
said. 'But another way of looking
at it is that we were the last team
who failed to beat Yugoslavia.
The lads played splendidly but
after all we had one victory and
that was against Zaire.

'When you compare all the
self-satisfaction at home with
what is happening in Brazil, it's a
bit sobering. Their national side
have a staggering record and,
even at this time, when they were
only a shabby imitation of their
old selves, they got to fourth
place in Germany. Yet while our
people are in a mood to erect
monuments, theirs are burning
effigies. Their reaction is ridi-
culous but so, in the opposite
way, is ours.

'The fellows who played for

"Never watch a game all year, but come Cup Final Day and it's a bleedin' social occasion."

Scotland out there did us proud and some back-slapping is in order but even by our own emotional standards we are getting a bit carried away.'

He is right but, as he admitted, getting carried away is a Scottish tradition. If, however, the Scots are serious about building on this year's accomplishments there must be a sensible and specific assessment of the performance in West Germany, a clear-eyed separation of the good from the bad, both on the field and in the vital area of preparation for the challenge.

That there were substantial deficiencies in practical appreciation was sharply demonstrated by the fact that when Scotland went out to meet Brazil neither the manager nor (more understandably) his players realised that the presence of Mirandinha in Zagalo's line-up meant Jairzinho would play on the right flank. Ignorance of this implication, which should have been plain to anyone who

had taken the trouble to find out that Mirandinha is purely and simply a central striker, threw Willie Ormond's team into dreadful confusion for 20 minutes or so and could well have cost them two or three goals.

Mr Ormond—who is, at the level of personal relations, one of the most appealing figures to be encountered in football—has always stressed that he is more concerned with 'getting my own team right' than with making a detailed scrutiny of the opposition's strength and defects.

It is true that the first priority with any team, and above all with any Scottish team, must be the organising and deployment of their own resources and the generating of a collective mood that would give maximum impact to their talents. But in a competition like the World Cup it would be almost impossible to succeed without a thorough awareness of the problems your rivals are likely to cause and of the questions

95

they in turn might be unable to answer on the field. Soldiers might develop toughness and high morale on manoeuvres in Glencoe but they would not be expected to do well in Vietnam without knowing something of the methods of the Vietcong.

Any reflections on the disciplinary troubles that afflicted the Scotland party on the approach to the World Cup should probably centre on the Celtic capacity for self-destructive behaviour. Yet, as one of the most authoritative observers of Scottish football suggested to me, the difficulties could have been lessened if the squad chosen had included more players who were genuinely in contention for places in the team.

'There was too much dead wood, too many fellows who were there to make up the numbers, to take up bed space,' he said. 'The result was that there were several men in the side who knew they were sure of their place, that wee Willie would be weakening his own position disastrously if he left them out. When you get lads in that situation, not only is it difficult for the manager to discipline them, it is difficult for them to discipline themselves. They are not restrained by the knowledge that their places could be in jeo-pardy and, even without meaning to, they can become lax with themselves.

'Every footballer who went on that trip should have represented a real alternative to a man in the first team.'

The same observer thought it was hopelessly bad planning that put the SFA officials in the same hotel as the players. 'Sometimes when I walked in there it was like an old folks' home,' he said. 'I felt I should be carrying a basket of fruit or a bunch of flowers. The officials should be separated from the men who have gone there to do a job of work. And the punters should not be allowed to swarm around the place as they did at the Scottish camp.

'Even the press should have only limited access, full co-operation for perhaps two half-hour sessions each day but not freedom to come and go as they like. Willie Ormond is such a nice fellow, such a warm wee man that restrictions of this kind probably don't come naturally to him but I think they are necessary.'

It is hard to disagree. With a lot more of such constructive criticism, the Scots may put themselves in a position next time to celebrate a victory rather than a thrillingly honourable failure.

From *Sportsworld*, 1974

24

All Mod Cons

Michael Parkinson

One thing his detractors can never accuse George Best of is not heeding their advice. They urged him to get married and he got halfway there, they warned him about 'burning the candle at both ends' and, from time to time, he extinguished at least one flame. He was told to forget his business interests and concentrate on his football which he did so frequently that his agent had to spend most of his time looking for his client.

Best knew better than most that such advice was mere sophistry when applied to his own case. But at least he went through the motions.

Another specious piece of advice he received was to find a nice homely girl—nothing flash— buy a house and settle down. He rejected the first half as being totally out of character, but the part about buying a home of his own filled him with strange enthusiasm. He nearly convinced himself that a house was the answer to most of his problems. In fact, it became a monument to them. No single episode in his life

so illustrates the predicament he was in.

To begin with it wasn't just a simple matter of building a house and then walking through the front door. He had first to get the permission of the club. Like most footballers, and certainly all Manchester United players, he was bound by contract to live in digs until he was married! It didn't matter that Best was earning £50,000 a year, that he was an international star, that he was inevitably forever on display and therefore in need of a retreat.

They were adamant that Best should live with Mrs Fullaway on a council estate in Chorlton and park his Rolls-Royce in the street outside.

For a long time, of course, Best had ignored the rule. To all intents and purposes he lodged at Mrs Fullaway's. In fact he slept in more beds than a travelling salesman and several restaurants in Manchester would have been in difficulties had he stopped eating out. But he was tiring of the nomadic life and wanted a proper home.

Typically he set about providing one without asking the club's permission. Originally he felt he needed a house in the country, an old cottage in fact. Then he settled for a house of ultra-modern design to be built on a site at Bramhall, a 'desirable' suburb of Manchester with the virtue of being near to the Club and the airport.

It was the kind of site a young company executive would choose to give himself easy access to town and to provide his family with a glimpse of the countryside. It was these same virtues—easy access from town and a glimpse of the distant Pennines—that were to make the site one of Britain's most popular tourist attractions—once the house was built and the new owner was in residence.

But even before that happened George Best's house was news. From the very first announcement that he was thinking of having a house built to the moment he moved in, what was designed as his private retreat had become public property.

A local architect, Frazer Crane, was given the job of designing Britain's most sophisticated bachelor pad. Crane's finished building was constructed on two levels with the main living areas of the house on the first floor. The ground floor had a spacious garage entrance, a billiard room and a bedroom and bathroom for the resident housekeeper. Upstairs was the main living room described by Best at the time,

'The second most important room in the house. I wanted a spacious interior where I could relax, entertain and listen to music.' The room was L-shaped and enclosed on two sides by floor to ceiling glass panels.

It gave a lovely view of the Pennines, it also gave day trippers a lovely view of George Best.

The bedroom where he now did most of his best work, incorporated a bathroom with a plunge bath large enough and deep enough to warrant an attendant, done in red and white mosaic — Manchester United's colours. Outside, the house had a mature orchard and a goldfish pond.

Just before he moved in Best was quoted as saying, 'When I get home I want something restful and soothing. I suppose it is because my life is frantic and noisy and I want a home which is a complete contrast.' In fact he would have been more private living in a floodlit phone booth, as he soon found out.

He moved in around about the autumn of 1970 without demur from the club which by now had settled into a policy of letting George do just about anything he wanted so long as he turned out for them on Saturday. The event did not, however, go unremarked by the press.

The Times gave a half page to a description of the house based on the premise contained in the opening sentence of the article, 'What happens when a twenty-three year old footballer decides

"It's my husband - quick put this on!"

to commission a firm of architects to design his first house?'

The snobbism inherent in that remark was mild compared with another report in the 'Daily Mirror'. I reprint it in all its pristine glory.

'Sunday trippers in their hundreds turned up yesterday to see the house that George Best built. The visitors peeped through the windows, gazed into the fish-pond, tramped around the garden and climbed the outside verandah stairs to get a closer look.

'And in the end most of them reached the same embarrassing conclusion about the white tiled residence in Blossom Lane, Bram-hall, Cheshire.

'It reminded them of a loo.

'The Manchester United soccer idol was away for the day from his new house designed to his own specification and reputed to be costing him more than £35,000.

'One of the visitors, Miss Ethel Deakin, 39, of Manchester Road, Burnage, Lancs, said, "It's lovely inside, but outside it's just too much. I was told I couldn't miss it because it looked like a public convenience, and I agree."

'A dog brought along by one of the visitors obviously agreed too. It eyed George's gleaming tiles, deliberately raised his leg and took a liberty.'

The 'News of the World' ran a competition for their readers to name the house. They received a thousand fit to print and from these George discarded any to do with soccer such as 'Off-side', 'Left - wing', 'Soccer - Haven', 'Goal Holme' and the like and chose 'Che Sera'. Miss E. Bradley, of Manchester, received £10 for her inspiration.

The 'Daily Express' persuaded Best to let them pay for the house-warming party in return for ex-clusive rights. Richard Taylor and Elizabeth Burton said they couldn't make it to Bramhall, as did Tony Curtis and Pierre Trudeau. Harold Wilson declined on behalf of Mary and himself but added: 'Delighted to see you're in such splendid form again, but to hit the crossbar from 35 yards in the last five minutes is a bit much.'

Tommy Trinder did arrive. 'I remember this place when it was the Odeon,' he told the reporters waiting outside the building. Imogen Hassall, who never misses a premiere, was another guest, as were several other nubile young ladies—including Misses United Kingdom and Great Britain—whose sole contribution to the evening was to push their breasts and bare their teeth at the 'Daily Express' photographers who worked throughout with the detachment of anthropologists observing the mating habits of a group of tipsy chimpanzees.

George Best went to bed early, not, it must be said, in protest at the guest list but rather in support of it.

Dick Best, his dad, caused a minor furore by announcing a preference for Guinness when offered champagne. Three security men controlled the doors and outside policemen patrolled to control crowds and traffic. Later these same policemen were the subject of an official investigation following a complaint that a panda car was used to carry drinks from a public house to the house-warming party.

The investigation came to naught except that George Best's house-warming became a matter for public controversy rather than private enjoyment.

The most that can be said for his first few weeks in residence is that at least it provided a change. The worst was that the publicity the house had been given—publicity which always included the address—soon gave it the appeal of a stately home.

Bus loads of sightseers started arriving from all over England. The slightly better off would bring the family car, park it nearby, and sit all afternoon gazing at the smoked glass windows of George Best's lounge.

Best recalls: 'It was unbelievable. After a few weeks I wished I was back in digs. At least a council house in Chorlton was harder to find than my place. i'll never understand why people came and just sat there hour after hour gawping at a house. I don't know if they expected me to stand up and give them a quick flash or something.

'There were always some people around no matter what day but Sundays were the worst. I thought at one time of opening a little stall selling cups of tea, sandwiches, hot dogs and the like. Or charging a parking fee. If I went out on a Sunday I could never get back in. I used to have to ask them to move their bloody cars from the approach to my house.'

The longer he stayed, the more intolerable living at 'Che Sera' became. His fishpond with its fifty goldfish had to be replenished after every weekend. Best wondered who was taking them and the mystery wasn't solved until a local teacher rang him to say that a gang of lads were selling George Best's goldfish every Monday at the school.

The teacher was not offering restitution, he was simply querying the validity of his pupil's claims.

A man came and left an armchair on George Best's front lawn. Best was tempted to release a news story saying that he had found £500 in pound notes concealed in the chair. 'With any amount of luck that would have given the bastard a heart attack,' he said.

The women were the worst. 'I used to get all sorts of women at the door. I'd get women who came during the day saying their daughters had pictures of me all over their bedroom walls and could she bring the daughter to the house so I could tell her not to be so daft. Then I'd get the young girls arriving at the door. If I liked them I'd have them in. If I didn't I'd tell them to shove off. I had two sixteen year-olds used to arrive regularly. Used to tell their parents they were going to the Youth Club, then come to my place. You wouldn't believe what they got up to.

'Then I had a bird used to drive up from Leicester every week. Married she was and wanted me to sleep with her. Never did because she was really ugly. They used to make all kinds of excuses to get in the front door. They'd ring the doorbell and when I answered it they'd say, 'Oh, is Mavis in?' And then they'd say, "Oh, aren't you George Best?" All that shit used to go on.

'The best was a blonde girl who arrived once and said, "My car's just broken down outside your house. Can I use your phone to call the AA?" I let her in because she was a fair looker. Then I had her on the carpet in the hallway before the AA men arrived. Gave her a quick repair job.

'In the end it got on my fucking nerves. I'd open my bedroom curtains in the morning and there would be a line of young birds looking through the window. It got so I wouldn't answer the phone. I had an Ansaphone installed. When the doorbell rang I

used to stay quiet and pretend I wasn't in and I used to hide be-behind curtains so the rubber-neckers couldn't see through the windows.

'It was mad. I became a prisoner in my own bloody house. I wanted to turn the whole bloody thing round so I faced away from the road and so they couldn't see me. Sort of turn my back on them.'

Instead of having the rehabilitative effect on Best that his advisors intended, the house undoubtedly emphasised his predicament and increased his frustration and anguish. He went back to his nomadic life, living in friends' flats, coming back to 'Che Sera' only when he had nowhere else to go.

From the moment he went to live there he began his rapid descent downhill.

He sold the house for £40,000 when he retired from football.

It was advertised as 'ex-soccer player George Best's luxurious house'.

Today he lives in digs with Mrs Fullaway and parks his Ferrari in the road outside.

From *George Best*, 1975

25

Football Fever (2)

John Moynihan

'So you had a lousy steak,' said our Mexican guide. 'Well, you go on and tell your agency. I'm only your guide.' We were a group of English football spectators travelling from Guadalajara to Mexico City, a twelve hour bus journey across pale mustard-coloured deserts and cactus lands flattened under an ominous blue sky full of puffy, motionless clouds.

England were already out of the 1970 World Cup, beaten by West Germany in the quarter-finals at León. We had seen the Brazilians perform wonders in Guadalajara, we had seen Gordon Banks's incredible save from Pelé. Some of us had crossed other sinister deserts to León and had almost wept as fat German butchers and bakers celebrated Gerd Muller's winning goal after extra time with flagons of Teutonic brewed ale. It was time to move on from west to east.

Twelve hours is a long time to sit in a bus. It is even longer, crossing a Mexican landscape. Lone yachtsmen can go silently barmy enduring days and nights on a flatulent ocean, and our own thoughts shifted and wavered dizzily as if we were at sea ourselves. The bus groaned on, climbing towards the Mexican capital where the final would be held the following Sunday. Three self-pronounced West Bromwich supporters were sleeping behind me with their mouths open, their open-neck, short-sleeved beach shirts moist with perspiration. One of them, Eddie, told me that he had never been out of England. 'I'm getting married soon, but the bride said it was OK. I came on this trip instead of going on honeymoon. She understood, it's only once in a lifetime.'

Eddie was one of 6,000 England supporters who had made the trip, and it had cost him about £300 basic to do so. He·was a typical representative from the United Kingdom, rather overweight, with a beer tummy, tubby legs, greasy jowls, a shrill metallic voice and a penchant for draught lager, bird talk, soccer and cards.

Now Eddie was dozing thousands of miles from home with his two chums, Taffy and Joe. He worked in a car factory and had saved up for two years to make the trip. It had not, as he would often say in the days ahead, gone 'all that roit, loik'. The food for a start. It was the hash-brown potatoes at his motel. It had given him a gippy tummy.

Eddie had lain spellbound and supine for five days with the worst tummy attack he had ever known. One or two informers had looked into the tiny chalet room he shared with Taffy and Joe and asked him how he was getting along. 'Pity you have to miss the Rumanian match, Eddie,' they said. It was diabolical. 'I just lay there wishing England along and hoping and then the lads came back and said Geoff Hurst had seen us through. And I got up cheering for a pint, like, then crumpled back on my ankles in the bar, like, and Taffy had to help me back all shivering and shaking.' A classic case of Montezuma's revenge, of course, but it was doubtful whether Eddie had been warned about this at his works. Footballers, officials, journalists came injected and doctrinated about the foreigner's curse in Mexico, but many an honest man came out without a clue of what it is like to travel abroad and the dangers of drinking the local water.

There they all were dozing and snoring in the bus now with the driver almost asleep himself as he faced the puffy clouds hanging over the dusty highway; the odd snore whipped up from the midriff of the bus. From Stepney and Liverpool 8, from Poplar and Newcastle, from Dorchester to Carlisle; the odd sombrero breezily lying on nodding foreheads, the odd cowboy hat tilted back, a bus boot crammed with suitcases overloaded themselves with bottles of Tequila, Mexican dolls, pottery, Aztec forgery, colonial bumph, Mariach LPs, frilly nightdresses for Paula and Sharon, teeny Christs from a souvenir-plundered church near León, beads and necklaces, woolly ponchos and Brazilian pennants. All these were coming with them to Mexico City.

Eddie groaned. He turned over so his chin fell against his right shoulder. He had come a long way, and that's what made him interesting. That bulky body transformed from a routine life and yet quite unaffected by the shock of change. He might have been sleeping in front of his own television set on a Sunday afternoon so uninfected was he about the landscape.

The guide had been right about the steaks offered to us with some reluctance two hours out of Guadalajara. Snowy, Jim and Pete from Liverpool had already tasted the prime cuts and sat with satisfied grins as we broke our teeth on ballbearing-lined strips of carcase. What had a travel brochure warned us before the trip: 'DON'T PANIC'? It is easy to panic in Mexico. Eddie chewed, belched, chewed. The meat reluctantly went down. Pete laughed: 'You ought to get here earlier, wack.'

A coach droning on the road— recent memories escalate: who else in the world but Pelé could have spied the Czech goalkeeper standing too far out of goal with his concentration at the ease position? Pelé was near the half-way line, and it only took him a fleeting second to respond to the Czech's lack of caution. He hit an instant shot which rose in the air towards our seats and came tumbling down past the goal-keeper to miss the near upright by a fraction and thump against the spectator barrier with the force of a charging bull. What was that old plant-grower from Norwich thinking of when he asked me if Pelé had headed or kicked the ball? Yet his absurd enquiry was not quite in the realms of fantasy as far as Pelé was concerned.

Match memories were suddenly distracted by the coach suddenly grinding to a stop half-way up a hill. Eddie was on his feet adjusting his slacks. The driver sat still without taking his hands off the wheel, the guide sat motionless, traffic surged on past. Eddie wanted to know what was going on. 'Oi—what's the matter?' Still no reaction—England supporters in the process of waking up all over the bus with tight-lipped yawns. Farmworkers in a far-off field motionless over their labours. A jet whirred over, high in the sky. The guide suddenly turned back at us, grinning with a thin trace of malice. 'Genmen—we have run out of gas. So sorry genmen.'

Eddie and his mates stood out-side the coach during the wait. We might have been on an outing to the Malvern Hills, or a jaunt to Blackpool with the lads lounging up against the coach smoking and mildly cursing the delay. The English have an ability to resist real irritation under mild threats of writing to their Member of Parliament or local newspaper about such inconveniences. Al-ready the travel agency which had brought our group was under fire for mismanaging accommo-dation, match tickets and meals. This new upset on the road only escalated men like Eddie's irri-tation, but it is not much use writing to your MP or local news-paper in the middle of a Mexican plain, where hawks fly high and mules gently doze. The Brazilian supporters would have started dancing on the roof of the coach with their drums and banners, the Italians would have wailed and pleaded during Caruso airs, the Germans would have stacked crates of beer outside the coach and burst into a Bavarian march-ing song, but here, in an unknown landscape, the English sat, bit their nails and waited. It was a long wait, but eventually the driver managed to flag down a lorry and syphoned off some petrol from his tank. The lorry driver grinned—it was a kindly act for unhappy gringos. And had we see Burby Cherlton? And Vinston Choichill? 'And England football no good now, I theenk. You go away early.'

'We're going to Mexico City, chum,' said Eddie, 'that's if they let us.'

Football supporters of the jet age, we drove on again, climball day until the silver skyscrapers of Mexico City fell below as the bus climbed to 10,000 feet, and then we drove round and round until we came to Cuernavaca where we would stay in a motel.

All was not well when we entered the town. A mildly randy couple from Wolverhampton were wandering round in the dark, looking for bed. Their motel had never got their booking and there was no room for them. They flagged our coach down in the centre of Cuernavaca, the old colonial town where Zapata started his revolution, and came pathetically aboard.

'We've been looking around some fields for somewhere to camp,' said the woman. She was still wearing a peaked cap decorated with a Union Jack and a photo of Gordon Banks but around her shoulders was a pink-green poncho.

'We've been all over town,' said her husband. 'Everything's shut up—you can't even get a beer.'

It was nearly midnight and we had been on the road all day. The driver stopped at a number of hotels dropping groups of supporters with suitcases. They departed, looking lost and tired, into white buildings covered with sensuous plants. When we reached our hotel, Eddie and his mates were first through the door into a brightly lit foyer full of sofas and ornate carpets. Some of our party were lucky, the man at the desk had rooms for them, but others would have to share with others, four or five to a room. There had, it seemed, been some mistake about bookings. Eddie was passionate about his stomach.

'Where the grub, chum?'

'Grub, meester. Grub?'

'Yes, grub, food, nosh.'

'We do not serve food here, mister. But there is a bowling alley if you wish.'

'Who wants a bloody bowling alley at this hour?' said Eddie. 'I want my dinner.'

'Sorry, mister. No food.'

The Wolverhampton couple found themselves a room, but Eddie never got his grub until the next morning. We sat into the early hours drinking beer and eating sandwiches scrounged from a nearby café.

'Look at him,' said Eddie, pointing out a Hampstead supporter who had managed to get himself an expensive meal. 'Scruffy little hairdresser—all stuck up, loik.' Eddie was keen to point out the social standing of his group. 'We are all working class here. Snowy, Jim and Joe, over there, come from Liverpool, Bill and Fred from London. Out here we are one common cause. We are united.'

Eddie's sense of being a member of a 'common cause', of being 'united', murmured back a hundred years to when his forebears began this business of travelling long distances to watch football matches in horse-drawn carts or on foot if they could not afford the train fare. It started in the

ANDY CAPP

Panel 1: YOU CAN'T SEND ME OFF JUST LIKE *THAT*—!

Panel 2: YOU 'AVEN'T PREVIOUSLY WARNED ME, BOOKED ME, CAUTIONED ME —

Panel 3: —AW, FORGET IT!

Panel 4: 'E *EXPECTS* ME TO SEND 'IM OFF — BUT THIS TIME IT WAS A BIT SOONER THAN 'E *THOUGHT* I WOULD

North of England with the arrival of the half-day Saturday when workers took time off to come 'Ooop for the Coop'. The first stalwarts came from Blackburn when they arrived in large numbers at the Oval in 1884 and were described in the *London Pall Mall Gazette* as 'a northern horde of uncouth garb and strange oaths'. This was probably the first full-scale invasion of a metropolis by a group of outsiders. Like the Brazilian supporters at the Jalisco Stadium, these Blackburn supporters let loose pigeons before a Cup Final in which Blackburn beat Queen's Park 2-1. The mood was set, and from then on, as soccer became more and more dominated by the professionals like Blackburn, Preston and Aston Villa, the masses rolled south to watch the game. Eddie's grandfather and father never went any further to watch West Bromwich, but it was a happy excursion; and even better if their team won, as they did against Birmingham in 1931.

'Dad talks about that day,' said Eddie. 'We got one up, then Birmingham equalised. Straight from the kick-off, we went right down the field and Richardson banged the ball into the net. We won 2-1. And he came down with me when we won the Cup in 1968. Bloody extra time, then Jeff Astle banged the ball in, what a rocket. We went down to Soho and got proper stoned.'

From *Football Fever*, 1974

26

Single-Minded

Jack Rosenthal

WINSTON PLATT'S *living room is festooned with Manchester City mementoes: photos of the team, a huge one of Colin Bell, City pennants, a blown-up cardboard cut-out of the League Cup on the sideboard, a City fixture list.*

WINSTON *is watching the last few seconds of an International football match on TV. He's perched on the end of the settee in total concentration. Sitting beside him, bored out of her mind, is his girl-friend,* NAOMI.

COMMENTATOR: And so goodnight to you—from International Football at Wembley. Goodnight. *Football sign-off music.*
WINSTON: (*Adoringly*) Colin . . . look at Colin, eh? (*Calling to the TV set*) Good lad, Colin, lad! (*Rhythmic hand-clap*) Eng-land!
NAOMI: (*Flatly*) Winston?
WINSTON: (*Chanting happily to himself*) We are the champions!
NAOMI: The whistle's gone, Winston.
WINSTON: (*Singing*) 'Oh, when the lads go marching in/Oh, when the lads go marching in/I want to - - -'

NAOMI: The game's *finished*, Winston.
WINSTON: Weigh up, Colin, though . . . Shaking hands with Eusebio. Bloody class, eh? It always tells. (NAOMI *gets up to switch off the set*) Naomi!!
NAOMI: It's over! Half the team's back in the dressing room!
WINSTON: Colin's *not*!
NAOMI: Sorry. (*She stands watching and waiting*) He's running off now, isn't he?
WINSTON: (*Twisting his head sideways to savour the last glimpse of his hero*) Like a bloody dream, that's all. (*Then, deeply satisfied*) OK.
She switches the TV off, then returns to sit next to him. He settles back, happily. NAOMI *gazes at him, admiringly.*
NAOMI: Don't you sweat when you get excited?
WINSTON: You probably thought Bobby Moore were playing a bit square at first—but he was only trying to overlap with his full-backs. Ramsey's picked that up from watching City.
NAOMI: (*Patiently, quietly*) Winston. Your mam and dad's gone to bed. I've still half an hour

before my last bus.

WINSTON: An odd cross-ball from Peters wouldn't have broken your heart, neither, would it? (*Accusingly*) He was starving Colin Bell, you know. Jealousy.

NAOMI: Sorry about this skirt. It always rides up when I sit down. (*She makes half-hearted attempts to pull it down, then hopefully*) Bringing out the beast in you . . .

WINSTON: Couple of weeks in City Reserves'd do Peters no harm . . .

NAOMI: Winston . . . I've been thinking . . .

WINSTON: 'course, the burning question now is will Colin be fit for City's match tomorrow night?

NAOMI: Winston, the burning question is where do I *stand*!

WINSTON: Important match. Newcastle at home. (*Shouting*) Up the lads!

NAOMI: (*Bitterly*) Hear, hear.

WINSTON: You what, love?

NAOMI: Winston. We've been going steady for nearly three months. I want to know where I stand.

WINSTON: Yeah.

NAOMI: Well?

WINSTON: What?

NAOMI: Pardon?

WINSTON: Did you say something?

NAOMI: (*Promptly getting up*) Goodnight, Winston.

WINSTON: See you, kid.

NAOMI: Is that all you've got to say?

WINSTON: Oh, no. No. 'course not. (*He thinks*) Thanks for seeing me home. (*Pause*) In time for the match, like. (*Pause*) Well, the highlights . . .

NAOMI: (*Heartbroken*) Goodnight. (*She exits*)

WINSTON: (*Calling*) Naomi?

She re-enters, brimming with renewed hope.

NAOMI: Yes?

WINSTON: (*Sympathetically*) Don't worry about it. Joe Mercer'll get Colin fit.

She slams out.

FADE DOWN.

From *The Dustbinmen*

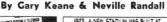

FOCUS ON FACT—*The Football Story (21)*   **By Gary Keane & Neville Randall**

1920. BIRMINGHAM. A MR. J. JERVIS BERNARD ISSUED COUPONS FOR 'COMBINATION BETTING' ON FOOTBALL MATCHES.

A YOUNG CABLE CLERK, JOHN MOORES, AND TWO FRIENDS PUT UP £50 EACH TO DO IT BETTER.

1923. THEY PRINTED 4,000 COUPONS. HIRED BOYS TO DISTRIBUTE THEM OUTSIDE MANCHESTER UNITED'S GROUND. CALLED THEM LITTLEWOODS POOLS.

A NEW FOOTBALL INDUSTRY WAS BORN, COLLECTING £200 MILLION, CONTRIBUTING £2 MILLION A YEAR TO THE F.A. AND LEAGUE.

1923. A NEW STADIUM WAS BUILT AT WEMBLEY FOR THE EMPIRE EXHIBITION TO HOLD 125,000.

A QUARTER OF A MILLION TURNED UP TO SEE ITS FIRST CUP FINAL. SWEPT THROUGH BARRIERS ON TO THE PITCH. DELAYED THE START FOR AN HOUR. BEFORE BOLTON BEAT WEST HAM 2-0.

27

Annual General Pantomime

Michael Carey

Derby County's annual meeting yesterday became the perfect tonic for the strife-torn world of football—an hilarious Christmas pantomime in one act. The leading characters were Baron Notsohardup (Sam Longson, the chairman), the impudent Buttons (Mike Keeling, a recently resigned director), Widow Twankey (a tetchy shareholder called Charles Cadman), and an audience who shouted and squealed with juvenile abandon. The Principal Boy was absent in Brighton and that seemed to be the cause of all the trouble . . .

Some people apparently could not get tickets and they stood outside the ground holding banners proclaiming 'Clough Will Return', and 'Board Will Relegate Us'. The drama started when Widow Twankey dumped a petition, condemning the board and bearing 7,000 names, in front of the Baron. He was quickly banished. Up jumped Buttons, who rapidly proved himself the master of the mischievous, questioning, for instance, travelling and match expenses.

'Just wake up and ask some sensible questions,' said the Baron, with some feeling. Buttons then got down to the real nitty-gritty. 'What about that time when we wanted the gutters cleaned?'

Voice from the audience : 'What are you trying to do? Let's get on with it.' (Shades of Nat Mills and Bobbie)

Someone then asked who were the three members of the Baron's staff who earned salaries in excess of five figures last year. The Baron said he was not allowed to answer that and then added that Brian Clough was one and Peter Taylor another.

There was a brief hiatus while a director was re-elected. 'Sydney, you're still very popular,' pronounced the Baron, sounding rather like Oliver Hardy.

Suddenly, and for no apparent reason, the Baron said his counterpart at Manchester United had telephoned him the previous night. 'I told him we were in bags of trouble and he said they were the same, what with O'Farrell leaving and Docherty coming, and some of their signings. He told me to stick to my guns and as an encouragement pointed out that their meeting lasted only seven minutes.'

The Baron then said he deplored the action of Derby's players recently. 'I won't say they were encouraged but they certainly were not discouraged,' he said. The protest movement, he added, had tampered with the players' careers which was very dangerous because they could have found themselves out of the game.

Dave Mackay (the new Principal Boy) was a man of guts and courage, he said, and would receive maximum support. As for himself, he had received letters comparing him to Winston Churchill, Golda Meir, and a Czechoslavakian leader whose name he gave up trying to pronounce at the third attempt.

Turning on poor Buttons, he said: 'If you say anything else I've got four men here who are going to pick you up and throw you downstairs and into the street and you can issue another writ against me.'

Widow Twankey then told the Baron he was not the man he was six years ago when he first took the Principal Boy from deprived Hartlepool to the luxury of Derby. 'He has never let you down,' he said.

Cries from the audience: 'Rubbish. Sit down. You're out of order.'

'Oh no, I'm not.' Chorus, even louder: 'Oh yes, you are.'

The Baron then revealed that his relationship with the Principal Boy had deteriorated two years ago. 'I sacked him three times and told him to b - - - - - off if he couldn't behave himself.'

Widow Twankey rose yet again. The Baron: 'Oh shut and sit down. Someone get hold of him. Get the police and throw him out.'

A young shareholder then said: 'The conduct of this meeting reflects no credit at all on the older generation. All I want to know are Mr Jack Kirkland's motives for acquiring so many shares.'

The Baron was ready for that. 'He's been a supporter all his life. Even used to do his courting in B stand. I think he fancied getting control of the club but I talked him out of it.'

Jeers and hisses from a certain section of the audience. But the hisses and boos at last turned to cheers when the new Principal Boy, a former member of the company in a more active role, took the microphone and said that Derby had the basis of the best team in the First Division, in his opinion, and he had made up his mind to make a success of the job over the next two years.

From *The Guardian*, 1973

28

Frankfurt, June 1974

Peter Cole

BEFORE...
Like a huge bubble hanging precariously on the end of the hand the child has dipped into her soap solution, there has grown up in Frankfurt this past week a fantasy of such extraordinary absurdity that it makes questionable the sanity of the thousands who believe it. The fantasy is that Scotland are not only capable of winning the World Cup, but that they will win it.

Rational analysis suggests that the bubble will burst at about 5.45 this afternoon when the whistle sounds the end of the game between Scotland and Yugoslavia. But rational analysis has never featured in the constitution of football supporters, and that was never truer than it is of the thousands of Scottish fans who fill Frankfurt today.

It is no exaggeration to say that they are completely dominating this town. In the week they have been here they have stamped their personality on what is normally a dreary place, effectively transforming the seedy Kaiser Strasse into an emigré Sauchiehall Street. The Germans, particularly the younger Germans, love it. Inhibition is clearly not a word contained in the vocabulary of the Scottish fan, they have brought a welcome dose of spontaneous enthusiasms, reckless optimism and totally unselfconscious joy.

There is an unintentional exclusivity about their high spirits. Nobody else can keep up with them. The Germans stand in little knots watching them, incredulous at the sight of the non-stop exuberance of the strangely attired men from Britain.

To the Scottish supporters themselves there is nothing British about it. They are as fervently nationalistic as any group of Scots I have seen. They jeer at the national anthem, wave their yellow and red lions Rampant or their blue. Last night they sang to the tune of We Shall Overcome 'Scotland will be free, some day.' They sang it with passion, louder than they sang their football songs.

By day the Scots laze around their camp-sites talking football. At night they take to the bars and sing football. In a country with an ostentatiously rich working class the Scotts appear tatty and poor. But it doesn't worry them at all. They have come to an expensive country with no more money than they would take on a day trip to London, but with well practiced guile they are working every fiddle in the book to keep themselves going.

The managers of the various camp-sites believe naïvely that they will be paid when the Scots leave, and there is hardly anybody on the camp-sites who is not a Scot. Many of them are down to their last few pounds—some have even taken jobs here—but miraculously there is always money for the evening's tribute to their football team.

The Scots have adopted the Sachsenhausen area of the town, an attractive district of narrow, trafficless streets and hot, crowded bars. They have selected the area because they are made welcome there and because the beer is cheaper than in the red light area they frequented at first. In the early hours of any morning one refrain echoes out of a series of bars, audible two hundred yards away. The Scots—who seem to feel a deep psychological need to remove most of their clothes whenever they are gathered together—are singing.

Hundreds of happy faces gaze towards a mythical day in early July when Billy Bremner and the team carry the World Cup back to Glasgow. Throw doubt on this preposterous idea and the fans look at you in blind disbelief.

'Six foot two, eyes a'blue, big Jim Holton's after you.' This is their favourite chant, repeated time after time all over Frankfurt. You hear it coming towards you long before the inevitable gaggles of kilted Scots round the corner. The strains can be heard long after they have disappeared from view. One Frankfurt paper printed the words in English, as a headline, and suddenly all the Scots, who cannot speak a word of German, were carrying the paper around, proudly showing it to anyone they met.

Even the few wealthy Scots who are staying at expensive hotels are as demonstratively football crazy as those on the camp-sites. For the last few days a huge Lion Rampant has hung from a twelfth floor window of the Inter-Continental Hotel which is the World Cup administrative headquarters during the tournament.

And yesterday in the plush and plastic hotel bar the organist who constantly provides eminently forgettable aural wallpaper swung into Scotland the Brave. Immediately a group of Scots was on its feet, dancing over the deep pile while dinner-jacketed waiters and expensively dressed guests stared in amazement.

Frankfurt's teenage girls are pursuing the Scottish fans. They wander into the bars in groups and unabashedly join groups of bare-chested boys in kilts. The supporters dance with them, talk to them in English in accents

"Too self-effacing to let on that he's come down to London to collect his Knighthood."

made the more obscure by drink and the girls laugh and make unsubtle advances. Clearly craziness has its attractions. But the best team in the world . . .

The tragedy is that such a devoted band of followers should have such a bloody-minded team which has spent its World Cup so far in niggling arguments with each other, the press, and commercial sponsors.

Perhaps if Willy Ormond took this team out into Frankfurt late one night to see the adoration expended on them by the thousands of fans, the players might be jolted out of their pitiful attitude to World Cup football. This afternoon is Scotland's big moment. There is not a Scot in town who believes it will be wasted.

AND AFTER . . .

Most Scottish football supporters were on their way home from here today, their spirits sapped by Scotland's failure to qualify for the last eight in the World Cup.

Frankfurt police and the British Consulate were relieved that the drunken frenzy which has been known to turn Scottish fans into violent thugs was evident to only a small degree.

The Scotland team, which returns to Glasgow tomorrow on a charter flight booked before it had played a game, made a major contribution to peace by scoring an equalising goal in the dying seconds of the match against Yugoslavia.

It dissipated the euphoria of the Yugoslav fans and gave the Scots a chance to say they had left the competition with dignity. Some convinced themselves that Scotland could well have won the World Cup.

So there was nothing to celebrate, and a self-induced feeling that there was no reason for a wake. Supporters waited by the team bus, gave their heroes a farewell cheer, and went quietly

114

away to try to get into the mood for a night's drinking.

Police and barkeepers were prepared for trouble, but had to cope with nothing more serious than a few drunks. No arrests were made. Most of the bars the Scots have filled for the past week closed rather than risk trouble, and many other bars refused admission to any Scot.

The most serious incident occurred just after the match, when a Yugoslav supporter was stabbed in the chest with a broken bottle. Several others were injured in the same fracas. The Yugoslavs greatly outnumbered the Scots at the match.

The British Consulate said it was very impressed with the Scots behaviour. It has had to deal with very few who have spent all their money, although at the Frankfurt camp-sites today many of the Scots said that they would have to borrow from the Consulate in order to get home.

The team drowned its sorrows until well into this morning at the Weilnauy Hotel, 25 miles outside Frankfurt, which is still under heavy guard after the supposed IRA threat last week. The players' spirits were clearly at a low ebb.

The police will be delighted when the team flies out, as protecting the Scottish players has been their greatest headache over recent days.

The most disturbing sight of the World Cup so far was the enormous helicopter flying low over the team bus as it made its way to and from the ground. The sides of the helicopter were open, and 14 members of Germany's anti-terrorist squad scanned the ground. All were holding rifles or machine guns at the aim position.

From *The Guardian*, June 1974

29

West Ham v. Manchester United

Julie Welch

'If you want to talk to me, my friend'—Tommy Docherty's hand shooed away an imaginary Irishman—'don't mention George Best . . .' It was after the game and the remorseless flak of his conversation had lost some of its customary brio. Behind him, his team gathered, spruce but chastened-looking. 'The lads did ever so well' Docherty continued. 'I thought we'd got it when the score was 1-1. It's a funny game. You don't get many laughs'.

Indeed what with Best on the transfer list again, United nestling glumly around the bottom of the First Division, and his team displaying a crudity of purpose that underlines how rattled they are, Docherty's situation ought to give him fewer laughs than a performance of Macbeth in a power cut.

United, or so one thought, had had it made. They were playing against a side not merely dispirited after midweek Cup defeat, but one peppered with strange young faces as West Ham took a peep at its long injury list and staggered backwards into puberty.

The story of the match was brief : two sides at the wrong end of the greasy pole trying desperately to clamber to safety and, in the case of Manchester United, not very particular how they managed it.

Forsyth was booked, and soon after, the threatening drudge Holton, some of whose tackles looked about as uncomfortable as a blind date with a mechanical plough. Macari and Kidd had Day trembling once as Coleman and Taylor gave them the run of the goalmouth ; both jumped over the ball instead, and McGiven got it way. That was about all the first half afforded, and Houston went off on the whistle with a bleeding nose.

The second half saw West Ham suddenly galvanised. Bonds deserved the forty-seventh minute goal ; he had shone so consistently in an otherwise dark game that one suspected he had a private generator of his own. Paddon took a throw in on the left, neatly ducking the attentions of Forsyth. Best headed the ball down to Bonds, who was lurking just outside the penalty area; he sent a long, low shot through a herd of bodies, one which Stepney could have hardly seen.

Kidd had contributed little to the game, and in the fifty-second minute he trooped off dispiritedly, to be replaced by McIlroy. The effect was fairly immediate. It was Wooler's mistake; a bit of defensive ineptitude which gave McIlroy the ball and a lot of time in which to crump the ball high into the net above Day's flailing limbs. Easy.

And so it was, almost, when Day only just managed to kick Young's shot off the line, and when Taylor performed a similar desperate lunge from a shot by Greenhoff, United suddenly looked a lot healthier. The entire West Ham defence grouped around their goalmouth and bobbed and kicked like latter-day Television Toppers until the final United corner was grabbed out of the air by Day.

The narrowest shave, though, went to McIlroy again. It was almost the move which brought him his goal; on the right, a little way out, and a shot which had Day whistling onto the ground, jabbing the ball against the post, and out. Out meant Macari, who had an open goal in front of him when he spooned that rebound into the crowd.

That was the end of United's period of cohesion. With West Ham cementing their game together again, Paddon took another corner which flew away from the crowded conditions in goal and into the clearer air round Holland's head. Defenders whirled, Stepney couldn't see, and the last stop before the goal was Best. He was on the line, and looked about as moveable as a London bus, but stepped aside politely to let Holland's header in.

Afterwards, Ron Greenwood looked almost as happy as a royal wedding. 'That's what life's about,' he said, a propos his younger players. 'If you give someone a chance they appreciate what you've done, and they pay you back tenfold. A spirit has come to life in the club—the sort of spirit to save us.'

'And you're out of the bottom three now?' someone added.

Greenwood beamed, just slightly maliciously. 'I understand so. I understand so.'

WEST HAM UNITED: Day: Coleman, Lampard, Bonds, Taylor, Wooler, McGiven, Paddon, Lutton, Holland, Best.
MANCHESTER UNITED: Stepney: Forsyth, Houston, Greenhoff, Holton, Buchan, Morgan, Macari, Kidd, Young, Graham. Sub: McIlroy.
Referee: R.N. Perkin (Stafford)

From *The Observer*, 1974

30

The Referee (The Football Man)

Arthur Hopcraft

'I've been pig sick when I haven't got a game I thought I ought to have had. I've had to run the line sometimes for someone else when I thought the game was mine by rights. I've said to myself afterwards, 'I could have eaten this kid—*eaten* him.' But I've still gone to him and shaken his hand, and said, "Well done, son." Well, that's sport. Of course it is.'

The football referee who said that to me revealed much more than the fact that he thought he had not always been sufficiently well rewarded for his sweat. He was speaking for the side of the referee's character which passes barely noticed by either the players or the fans: his place as a competitor in the game.

In English football there are between 15,000 and 20,000 referees. They include boys of sixteen and middle-aged men with paunches and inadequate spectacles. Thousands of them never rise above the lowest class of football in those lumbering Sunday afternoon games on the public recreation grounds which ooze tuftily between the lines of council houses and the ring roads. For thousands more there is, at least at some point in their lives, the real hope that they will win their way through' to the *elite* eighty, the ones appointed as Football League referees. A few hundred reach the looming obstacle before that happy goal, which is to be accepted as a League linesman; it is from the linesmen that the final promotion to League referee is made.

Referees regard selection for the most glamorous matches, such as FA Cup Finals and international games, with every bit as much longing and pride as do players. The secretary of the Referees' Association talks about the privilege of 'treading the Wembley turf' with as much awe as I have ever heard from any a player. Referees suffer from tension before and during matches as players do; they admit to jealousy and vindictiveness in their fraternity; they become minor celebrities; they receive letters of praise and sour abuse from people they have never met. They see themselves as part of the

118

"Play on, having your shirt torn doesn't mean a thing."

action, closer to it than managers. Just as with the players, it is when a referee stops getting letters and is no longer being cheerfully booed outside football grounds that he worries most about his future.

On the face of the matter the referee in top-class football is an anachronistic figure. He is still a part-timer, in fact very nearly an amateur, controlling a match in which the player's wages often total £2,000 and the result of the game may hinge on his decisions. Yet he undergoes only a minimal degree of formal training; in many cases he spends the rest of the week in a position of little importance in some employer's office; and he is paid £10.50 a game, with a choice of sixpence a mile or his first-class train fare for travelling, a maximum allowance for meals of £3 and an extra £4.20 if he has to stay overnight in a hotel. While football has changed dramatically in terms of pace, competitiveness and anxiety for reward, it is still controlled on the field, where it matters most, from the ranks of the clerks and shopkeepers and foremen who turned to the job when they realized, regretfully, that they would never be competent as players.

There are a few League referees with substantial professional qualifications in their everyday careers and some who run their own businesses; but of the best of them most have had to subordinate ambition, or even effort, in their regular work in order to blow the Acme Thunderer, the standard British referee's whistle, in professional football. Because of the increased speed of the game and the close critical attention nowadays given to refereeing it is accepted that unless a man has reached the League's list of linesmen by his early thirties he will never referee a League match. Every referee must start at the lowest level, and in order to work his way up the promotion ladder, through the town and regional leagues, he must start at the latest before he is out of his early twenties. The League fixes the retiring age at forty-seven.

Maurice Fussey is one of the League's best known referees, attracting attention as much for the obvious jokes that his name invites as by his arresting appearance. He is a tall, galloping-major type of figure, with sparse, sandy hair and a sandy moustache kept uniformly trimmed. Off the field he is relaxed and affable, attentive to questions and ready with inoffensive little stories about the quirks in the characters of famous players and other referees. 'Did you know there's one referee who always takes a hot bath twenty minutes before a game?' he said to me. 'I always tell him it can't be a good thing for his health, but he says it's the only thing that relaxes him.' In action on the field Fussey moves with unforgettable mannerisms.

He is famous for his furious sprints to the scene of dramatic incident. His white knees pump high, and his elbows piston so that his clenched fists jab up and down beside his chin. He is a picture of urgency: authority in a state of tizzy. The crowd often laughs or hoots in encouragement or derision, according to how his decisions have been going for their team. Fussey does not resent this response. For one thing it takes a little of the tension out of the atmosphere. For another his first concern is to reach the spot of the ruction as suddenly as he can manage it, and he does not care that his style is ungainly. He said : 'The thing is that when you blow your whistle for a foul the player's immediate reaction is to turn round and look at you. It's instinct. Now, if you're twenty yards away he's going to argue, because he's got time. But if he turns round and you're right behind him, even if you've just arrived, he's going to think twice.'

Referees are involved in the sweat and rancour of the game. They are close to the pain and the outrage which can only be observed distantly, and for that reason imprecisely, by the crowd. Referees are conscious of what players are saying to each other. They can watch the bitterness develop in a match long before the crowd sees its explosive result.

Referees like to feel that they are respected by players for their astuteness and their fairness ; they are, in this respect, like schoolteachers who regard themselves as close to the boys, or police detectives who think that give-and-take with criminals is the best way to deal with them in the long run. Fussey expressed this attitude explicitly when he said, with evident pleasure and pride, that a certain Scottish international player, known for his unpredictable temper, 'doesn't bear me any ill will because I sent

"Steady lad we've got three more sweaters and a see-through bra before the whistle goes."

him off'. He was confirming the same attitude when he said that another temperamental international 'responds to the right treatment'. This man, he said, was 'a great character, really, and it's no use making a lot of threats'. By and large, Fussey said, he found professional footballers were a 'great crowd', which is generous of him, considering the low opinion players are often prepared to give of referees.

It is striking how closely referees align themselves with players, in contrast with the scorn with which players will detach themselves from connection with the referees. There is no question about who would like to change places with whom. It is a romantic and, it seems to me, most unrealistic view of refereeing to say, as Sir Stanley Rous, the President of FIFA (the international football authority), says: 'It is a job for volunteers, who are doing a service to the country.' Plainly it is not public spiritedness that motivates men into the ambition of controlling big football matches, even if the authorities insist on treating them like servants of duty. As with managers and directors there is undoubtedly a deep absorption in football here, and the material reward is insubstantial to say the least of it. But there is much more satisfying of ego than disinterest in the motive. The referee wants to be recognized in the game, and he wants to feel he is important to it. He even wants to be liked.

Success as a referee requires devotion to the job. A League referee has to keep himself at a level of physical fitness which is far beyond the reach of the average man of his age. In his forties he has to try to keep close contact with the eye of the hurricane in the game, hard on the heels of the central action all the time. A breathless referee is a flustered and inadequate one, open to abuse from the players and hardly in a position to subdue it. Rous insists that it is vital to the game that 'we should get back to the position we used to have, when players always accepted the referee's decision as final'. The point is that some referees command that degree of submission from players and some are clearly not worthy of it. Fussey, like other leading referees, places physical fitness first in his order of essential attributes for effective refereeing.

He is a bachelor with a clerical job with the National Coal Board, and his life is centred on football. He trains two evenings and four lunchtimes a week, mostly at Doncaster Rovers' ground, and on the one Saturday in five when he does not referee a League match he trains in the morning and either watches or referees schoolboy football in the afternoon. He began refereeing when he was twenty-one, and it took him eleven years to reach League matches.

Fussey said he was seldom conscious of crowd reaction, and only occasionally did spectators' abuse get through to him. It needed a lull in the general clamour for the word 'bastard' which was the most frequent epithet to burn a way through his concentration on the game.

Off the field he wears a large Football League badge on his blazer. Outside grounds on Saturdays, or in the street during the week, he said, people often stopped him to say something like: 'Oh, I remember you. You gave so-and-so a penalty in the Cup in 1962. We'd have won but for you.' The arguments he was mostly called on to settle were those about interpretation of the offside rule. (This rule obsesses some referees as well as spectators. One League referee has named his house 'Offside'.)

Fussey said he was aware of tension at matches but did not think he was unsettled by it. 'But once you step out there you know there's only you who can make the decisions. That's real responsibility, and I feel it. I don't deny it.' When he entered refereeing he was keenly interested, but not immediately imbued with ambition, he said 'But once I realised I was making progress I knew I had to be a League referee. That was when I got stuck in and really did it properly.'

He named two other qualities for successful refereeing to accompany fitness. A referee ought always to be well turned out, he said, and he had to be naturally tactful: that is, he must not be subject to an impulsive attitude in moments of stress, because it immediately angers people. (Is this not the good policeman again?)

There is a standard uniform for League referees consisting of black shorts and shirt, and Fussey said that people were more likely to defer to a man whose uniform was always clean and well pressed. He said: 'It makes him look as if he's going to take it seriously. You're not going to have respect for him if he's in a dirty pair of shorts and some scruffy old shirt.'

The part-timer who disciplines the professionals is in turn judged by the amateurs. The two teams' directors have to report to the League after every match on the referee's performance. Literally, they 'mark his card'. They are required to score the referee on a scale of nought to ten. (At the start of the 1970-71 season the League introduced a system of second opinions on referees' efficiency: an assessor, always a former referee, is now at each match to score the official on the same scale.)

Referees are divided on the value of this system. (It is not optional to the clubs; they can be fined £5 for failing to submit a report.) The most self-confident referees tend to defend it by silence, dimissing the matter with the observation that good referees have nothing to be afraid of. Others attack the arrogance of the procedure. Some point to the absurdity of being judged by directors of a team which may have had a couple of penalties awarded against it. The argument in favour of the system says, in effect, that between the views of the most disgruntled of directors and those of the most pleased a reasonable mean of a referee's ability emerges over the months. But again the point is glaring that there is a vast difference in attitude between the intense preparation of players to contest the game and the crude, rule-of-thumb manner in which authority oversees it. There is absolutely nothing in the League's regulations which guarantees that the directors who are assessing the referees actually know the offside rule.

This is not to say, of course, that there are no clubs which have close connection with refereeing. There are retired referees who become directors, and there are clubs which frequently invite referees to talk to them and their supporters' clubs about the job. But neither the referees nor the League and the FA can influence the clubs in the attention they pay to referees' problems beyond the directors' own degree of interest. The referee is in the unsatisfactory position of a consultant brought in to adjudicate, instructed to brook no interference and then made subject to the criticism of his employers on the grounds that he was not up to the job.

Under these circumstances one of the English referees in the 1966 World Cup, Ernie Crawford, could hardly be said to be overstating the referee's predicament when he said that he needed, above all else, 'a skin like a rhinoceros and to be as deaf as a doornail'. Fire is breathed on him from the crowd, obscenity may be muttered at him by the players, and afterwards he can be accused of both laxity and over-zealousness, by directors watching the same game. As Crawford said to me: 'The referee's only got to make one bad mistake and everything else he does in the game is forgotten.'

Crawford reached retiring age after the World Cup, so when I talked to him at his home in Doncaster he was in the mood to review his career as a referee. It is hard to imagine a more explicit example of a competitor in sport suddenly shoved aside by the years. It was his voice I quoted at the beginning of this chapter, remembering his bitter disappointment at not being chosen for a top game. But his years as a referee had their moments of high flame, as well. He said: 'When you get a letter from Lancaster Gate (the FA headquarters) saying you've been picked to referee a game like England versus Young England, well, the walls move in and out and you could rush outside and kiss people in the street. It's like being picked to play for England.'

Crawford, a tiny Yorkshireman with the unnerving vibrato of the drill instructor in his voice, refereed in ten countries and never thought it necessary, or even relevant, to conceal how much he had enjoyed the glamour and the drama of the exhilarating show-piece matches of international football. His only regret was that he had never taken charge of an FA Cup Final; but in his living-room he pointed out the shining cups and plaques which filled a glass-fronted showcase with a precise memory of each occasion they marked. He took me round the house, lingering at every souvenir with which it was hung. They decorated nearly every wall and corner. There were china plates, dolls, crystal goblets, a gold whistle, a cigar box, plaques and medals, an ornamented bull, vases. Most of them were gifts from foreign clubs or from rich football patrons whose names meant nothing to him. A delicate coffee set reached him from Italy, addressed simply: 'E. Crawford, The Referee, England.' When he refereed in an inter-clubs contest in Barcelona, which had no British connection beyond his own presence, the loudspeakers silenced the crowd with a full rendering of *God Save The Queen.* To mark his selection as a World Cup referee Doncaster Corporation gave him a blazer with the borough coat of arms on the breast pocket.

Crawford was a League referee for fifteen years. He turned to the job in response to the prompting of one of the elder statesmen of football in his area soon after he admitted to himself that he would never be able to make a living as a player. He remembers his first assignment as a referee in local football with the same cringing pain that some people show when they recall their first visit to a dentist or first fall off a rock face. The match was a local 'derby' between the two teams of the same mining village. 'It was the worst experience I ever had in my life,' he said. He awarded a penalty in the first five minutes. 'I put the ball on the spot and a chap came up and kicked it away. Well, I spoke to him nice and politely and said he shouldn't do that, and that was how it went on. I was dreadful. The game afterwards was just a shambles. I wanted to see a hole in the ground I could jump into. We changed in the pub, and when we got back there the comments were terrible. They paid me five shillings, and they made it up in all the threepenny bits and pennies and ha'pennies they could find. They followed me all the way to the bus, shouting at me.' He was twenty-two.

When he got home he immediately wrote to his mentor, saying that he had refereed his last game. He said to me: 'I told the wife, "I'm not having this, not for five bob a week."' But his anxiety to stay close to football was an ally to authority's persuasion, and his next match was the return encounter between the same teams, the decision made on the grounds that send high-wire men back up the rope ladder immediately after a fall. He said: 'The advice I was given was to wait for the first chap to open his mouth and then give him some stick. Well, this feller, poor chap, he didn't do anything really, but I tore this strip off him. He didn't know what hit him, and after that it was a wonderful game.'

Crawford reached the League at the time when professional football was still being played on Christmas Day, and he made the point strongly that the privations of referees at the time were far worse than the players' circumstances. A working man without a car in the early fifties, he had to make his own way to Christmas matches when public transport was skeletal. He said: 'This is what I meant by dedication. I've gone to bed at 8 p.m. on Christmas Eve so that I could be up to get the only train on Christmas morning. I've landed up at Chesterfield at 7.30 on Christmas Day, wandering about when there's no one around. I was huddling in this doorway when a policeman came up and wanted to know what I was doing. Well, he had a right. I told him who I was, and he took me off to his little kiosk and we had a cup of tea with some whisky in it. He said, "Well, I thought I had a lousy job, but yours is worse."'

Referees who have worked their way through that sort of thing are not likely to be reticent when they are offering their opinions on the ways other men should prepare themselves for the job. Crawford said he was a frequent speaker at referees' gatherings, and he did not think it could be drummed home too often to them that if they were ambitious they had to train without stint. He said: 'I've run round Doncaster Rovers' track in pouring rain with a towel round my head, when the weather's been so bad that the players have been kept inside for talks.' A referee also needed a sense of humour; he would never succeed if he was pompous; finger-wagging and elaborate lecturing of players could irritate more than control. He said, 'I don't know how many players I've sent off. I don't want to know. It's one of the easiest decisions to make, to send a man off. That's not what you're there for. The hard thing is to keep him on sometimes. You do better keeping your voice down. I've run alongside players and said, "Ee, give over, I knew thee when tha was a good player." That hurts more than shaking your finger at a man.'

Crawford was an effective, obeyed referee, probably for the most part because he remembered his own belligerent nature as a young player and had the good sense to keep in mind the fact that youth, impetuosity and the burning will to win go together in a highly combustible package. He said he had been a 'bad lad' as an adolescent player. 'I'd kick anything above the grass,' he said. Recalling his own attitude to authority when he was the age of many of today's professional footballers, he emphasized that all referees should make it a rule never to touch a player. He said: 'A referee jabbed me in the chest once when I was playing, and he was the luckiest man alive. I could have kicked him in the teeth.'

This may not be the tone of voice which the government of football likes to hear. The leadership suggests, in its public utterances on the vexing problem of the growing dissatisfaction with refereeing, that it would prefer a more haughty detatchment by referees. This reflects a mistaken belief that the arrogance of authority, as exercised on the school playing field over a captive company, can be extended to the professional game as long as the official is enough of a disciplinarian. Crawford's attitude was that the players knew referees made mistakes; it was no use pretending otherwise. The task was to convince the players that the referee always 'gave what he saw'. Similarly a referee ought to be able quickly to differentiate between the spontaneous expletives of angered players and the malevolent abuse of those trying to intimidate him.

Sir Stanley Rous made his name as a referee before he became secretary of the FA and eventually president of FIFA. Admittedly the football Rous controlled was less explosive than today's, but he and Crawford were at one in the view that an adjustable deafness was a positive asset. Rous did not send off the French captain who once questioned the award of a penalty with a furious, 'Bloody *porquoi*?' Crawford said that there could be little future for the referee who regularly admitted being sworn at; too many complaints would put him in a similar position to that of a player who shows too readily how he can be hurt. Here again we have the point that the referee sees himself as part of the action, not an agent of authority.

Crawford found that the best team captains quickly understood how much it was in their own interests to support the referee; bitterness over a harsh decision might well linger in a captain's mind, but it was less dangerous to his own success than letting one of his men get sent off the field for intransigence. Crawford said: 'I've known a captain threaten to thump one of his own men for arguing with me. I always made a point of letting captains I didn't know very well understand exactly what I'd stand and what I wouldn't. I'd say to them "Right, now look, we're going to play football; that's why we're all here.' Captains always knew with me that they weren't just there for the toss of the coin.'

In a game which creates as much passion and as much demand on a man's resources as does professional football there are bound to be moments when gamesmanship and outright villainy test a referee to his limit. There are also times when he has to decide which of the two is present in the same incident. The good referee is not the man who plays safe with either a blind eye or a public display of moral outrage, but the one who can unobtrusively remove the teeth from the offence. The story goes that one famous referee awarded a penalty in the closing minutes of a cup-tie, when the score was 0-0. As the hot-shot of the visiting side prepared to take the kick the captain of the other team said softly in the hush of the moment: 'Bet you twenty quid you score.' The referee, equally softly, said to the villain: 'Bet you he takes it again if he doesn't.'

From *The Football Man*, 1968

FOCUS ON FACT —*The Football Story (22)*

By Gary Keane & Neville Randall

1928. FIFA DECIDED ON A CHAMPIONSHIP OF THE WORLD.

1930. FIRST WORLD CUP COMPETITION WAS STAGED BY URUGUAY, OLYMPIC FOOTBALL WINNERS. 13 TEAMS —NONE FROM BRITAIN—ENTERED. FINAL: URUGUAY 4 ARGENTINA 2.

1934. SECOND WORLD CUP IN MUSSOLINI'S FASCIST ROME. 32 ENTRIES —STILL NO BRITISH. ITALY BEAT CZECHO-SLOVAKIA 2-1 IN THE FINAL. CAME TO LONDON. LOST TO ENGLAND 2-3.

1950. ENGLAND ENTERED THE WORLD CUP—AS FAVOURITES. FLEW TO BRAZIL. WERE BEATEN 0-1 BY AMERICA, 500-1 OUTSIDERS. BECAME THE LAUGHING STOCK OF FOOTBALL.

FINAL: URUGUAY 2 BRAZIL 1.

FOCUS ON FACT —*The Football Story (23)*

By Gary Keane & Neville Randall

1953. EUROPE'S CURRENT TOP TEAM, HUNGARY, CAME TO WEMBLEY. TO PLAY ENGLAND STILL UNBEATEN AT HOME. PLAYED DAZZLING FOOTBALL TO WIN 6-3. THE MASTERS' FIRST HOME DEFEAT.

1954. FIFTH WORLD CUP IN SWITZERLAND. ENGLAND REACHED THE QUARTER-FINAL. THEN LOST 2-4 TO URUGUAY.

HUNGARY, UNBEATEN IN 30 PREVIOUS INTERNATIONALS OVER FOUR YEARS, MET OUTSIDERS GERMANY IN THE FINAL. AND LOST 2-3.

GERMAN CAPTAIN FRITZ WALTER.

1958. MANCHESTER UNITED, ENGLISH LEAGUE CHAMPIONS, ENTERED THE EUROPEAN CUP. BEAT RED STAR, BELGRADE. FLEW BACK VIA MUNICH. AND CRASHED.

EIGHT PLAYERS DIED: EIGHT WERE INJURED. THE FLOWER OF ENGLISH FOOTBALL WAS CUT DOWN.

31

The Groundsman

Ian Wooldridge

Wembley the morning after the England *v* Portugal match, was ten shades of grey.

Sheet water lay at the foot of the fortress walls. The flags, heavy as lead, clung round their poles for cold comfort. Rubbish still lay ankle deep on the chipped terraces.

Out on the pitch a thousand divot scars remained untended, filled with the unrelenting rain that was fast turning an historic battlefield into an urban swamp. The sour mood of the night before still hung around the great girders overhead.

It was not at all as Percy Young had planned it or dreamed of it or prayed that it would be. He is a houseproud man with an exactly symmetrical military moustache and no patience with union hours or those who invoke rule-books when there is still work to be done.

'I wanted a pitch of absolute perfection and I wanted to see England win on it in a glorious game,' he said. 'We didn't get either and I'm very sad about it.'

Young is 67 years old. He was appointed Wembley's head groundsman in May 1937 and has prepared the pitch for every Soccer international there between then and the day before yesterday.

As such he compares with the famous gardener at an Oxford college who was asked by a breathless American tourist: 'Say, how do you keep these lawns in such marvellous condition?

'Simply,' replied the gardener, 'by rolling and mowing them for 400 years.'

'Yes, I've heard of him,' said Young. 'He was absolutely right. A pitch needs care and love but it also needs expertise and money. Above all it needs time.'

Young who retires shortly and has also been responsible for speedway, greyhound racing and the 1948 Olympics at Wembley, has given seven days plus several evenings a week—80 hours on average—for $37\frac{1}{2}$ years to the cause.

He has always been paid a flat wage, without overtime. I take a liberty when I reveal that a winning Cup Final team once tipped him half a crown (12½p to new readers) in their hour of triumph.

He is an uncompromising man with a mistrust of reporters 'The last one who interviewed me,' he said, 'was so drunk that he had to lean against that wall (he pointed precisely to the spot) to stay upright long enough to ask his questions. Even when he put them I couldn't understand what he said.'

We managed passably yesterday but the Keeper of the World's Most Famous Lawn was discreet to the end.

Billy Wright was the friendliest footballer he ever met. Today's players, with their higher wages, 'didn't want to know the groundsman.' Sir Alf Ramsey was an ever-courteous, much-maligned man. The opening ceremony of the London Olympics, followed by the World Cup Final and the Matthews FA Cup Final were the three sporting occasions that all brought tears to his eyes.

The cruellest moment was when the Wembley authorities agreed to stage the International Horse Show on his sacred turf. In one week more than 30 years of work was destroyed and the 10,935 square yards of God's earth which he had nurtured with such tenderness had to be relaid.

One of the great moments came shortly before the kick-off against Portugal.

'Mr Revie asked me to come into the dressing room,' he said, 'and they presented me with a ball autographed by both teams. Mr Revie made a speech. I was overcome by the whole thing.'

What overcame him still more was the fact that, in the end, he could not provide England with the pitch he felt they deserved. 'We haven't had two consecutive days without rain,' he said, 'and the turf which had to be laid over the speedway track gave us no chance.'

The rain still drummed into the Wembley pitch as he spoke.

'I am retiring a mile up the road,' he said, 'to look after a 60 ft. front garden and a 75 ft. long back lawn. It's about time I did. My wife has been completely responsible for them for the past 37 years.

From *The Daily Mail*, 1974

FOCUS ON FACT —*The Football Story (24)*   **By Gary Keane & Neville Randall**

1962. WORLD CUP IN CHILE. A BRILLIANT BRAZILIAN TEAM BEAT ENGLAND IN THE QUARTER-FINAL. CZECHO-SLOVAKIA IN THE FINAL 3-1. TO WIN TWICE IN SUCCESSION.

A NEW MANAGER, ALF RAMSEY, WAS APPOINTED TO PREPARE ENGLAND FOR 1966.

1966. WORLD CUP FINAL AT WEMBLEY. WATCHED ON TELEVISION BY 400 MILLION. ENGLAND v. WEST GERMANY.

2-2. EXTRA TIME. HURST HIT THE CROSSBAR. SCORED A DISPUTED ENGLISH GOAL, AND ANOTHER IN THE LAST MINUTE TO MAKE IT 4-2.

1974. WORLD CUP FINAL AT MUNICH. TICKETS £200. TV AUDIENCE A THOUSAND MILLION. WEST GERMANY BEAT HOLLAND 2-1.

TWO DUTCH VIEWERS THREW THEIR SETS THROUGH THE WINDOW. ARMED GUARDS PROTECTED DEFEATED BRAZILIANS FROM ANGRY CROWDS. FOOTBALL FRENZY GRIPPED THE WORLD.

I

32

Goodbye to All That

Bernard Joy

Amateur status in soccer died on Monday January 23rd 1975, killed by its own hand.

Clubs and competitions can still use the word amateur in their titles, but as far as the FA are concerned, the distinction between amateurs and professionals will be scratched at an extraordinary meeting and all footballers will be known as players.

Instead of following the True Blue standards of Corinthians, Northern Nomads, Casuals and—in the 1950s—Pegasus, many leading amateur teams chose to be shoddy imitations of professionals—enticing and rewarding players with under-the-counter payments.

They took a road of subterfuge and hypocrisy which was so artfully concealed that the FA had no alternative to their present action.

Amateur internationals laughingly turned down League clubs whose offer did not match their earnings.

The adage that an amateur is 'not good enough to be a professional' became a cynical 'not offered enough to be a professional'.

The founders of the game would have been horrified that the principal amateur league, the Isthmian, whose motto is 'Honor Sufficit' should be sponsored by Rothmans while still officially amateur, and even worse get bonus payments for good sportsmanship.

For years the FA tried to eradicate the evil of illegal payments.

Skelmersdale were caught after winning the Amateur Cup in 1971 under the captaincy of Liverpool and Eire forward Steve Heighway and were fined £1,000. They turned professional the following season.

But cases were hard to prove—the example of Skelmersdale was not a deterrent—and in 1972 the move for abolishing amateur status was submitted to the FA Council.

Denis Follows, FA secretary at the time, commented: 'I have nothing but respect for professionals and no objection to people receiving money for playing football. What I object to is people being paid and evading tax. I don't like cheats and I don't like deception.

'We have been accused of shutting our eyes to a problem which we knew existed. The difficulty was to prove that there were illegal payments. What was our worry for so long now becomes the taxman's problem.'

We have already withdrawn from the Olympic Games which is dominated anyway by Iron Curtain countries Poland, Hungary, Russia and Yugoslavia, who blatantly field 'Government amateurs'—full-time state-employed athletes.

Amateur internationals have been suspended and the Amateur Cup replaced by the Challenge Vase.

It is a tragedy, because amateurs contributed so much to the development of football, fashioning a team game out of mob football before the FA was formed in 1863.

They were the first to win an international tournament for Britain—the Olympic title in 1908 and 1912—and gave shape to tactics.

They brought freshness and vigour and even today Isthmian League clubs produce giant-killing acts. This season Leatherhead beat Colchester and Brighton, while Wycombe restricted Middlesbrough to one goal in 180 minutes football.

These exploits follow those of Walthamstow, who drew with reigning Champions Manchester United at Old Trafford in 1953,

and Tooting, who beat Bournemouth and Northampton before going down to eventual winners, Nottingham Forest, in a replay in 1959.

Pegasus were a combined Oxford and Cambridge University side founded by FA vice-chairman Professor Sir Harold Thompson to encourage schools to play soccer.

They could not be assembled until after the Varsity match in December and trained together only on the Christmas tour.

Yet in their first season they reached the last eight of the Amateur Cup, and two seasons later, in 1951, they won the trophy, beating Bishop Auckland before 100,000 at Wembley.

Two years later they triumphed again, beating Harwich 6-0.

The players who stimulated the imagination of every genuine amateur in the country included county cricketers Doug Insole, Donald Carr and Tony Pawson, goalkeeper Mike Pinner, Jack Laybourne and John Tanner. Pegasus provided 14 amateur internationals during its six-year existence.

But there was an unfortunate side effect. They cut across the supply of players from the Universities to Corinthian Casuals, who were already losing players either for money or a better chance of honours elsewhere.

Old Blues no longer went automatically to Corinthian Casuals and chose clubs like Harwich, Enfield, Kingston and Wimbledon.

The Corinthian and Casuals

were founded as separate bodies in 1883 and amalgamated in 1939.

The Corinthians were formed to give leading English players practice together in order to counter the ascendancy of Scotland, who won eight of the previous nine matches against England.

Although professionalism was legalised in 1885, Corinthians continued to supply the bulk of the international side and England twice consisted entirely of Corinthians in the 1890s.

The results against Scotland took an upward turn, with nine victories in the next nine matches.

Their dash, daring and flair brought outstanding results against professional clubs, although they were not in the League and did not have a ground of their own.

They thrashed Blackburn Rovers, the FA Cupholders, 8-1, beat Preston 5-0 in the Northerners' Cup and League double year of 1889 and four years later had a 10-3 victory over Bury.

Players of the early days included C.B. Fry, the greatest ever all-round sportsman, and G.O. Smith. Between the wars were Graham Doggart, who became FA chairman, Norman Creek, high-jump champion Howard Baker, Jackie Hegan, who played against Millwall in the Cup with a broken tibia, and the Ashton brothers.

Incidents during a tour illustrate the standards Corinthians stood for. A penalty was awarded against them, and the captain ordered his goalkeeper to stand outside the goal while it was taken.

In the same match a penalty was given to Corinthians but as the captain considered the decision unfair, he kicked the ball into touch.

Nowadays he would be condemned for bringing the game into disrepute by showing dissent.

How the climate has changed in amateur football !

Tony Pawson tells of the instructions coach Vic Buckingham, later manager of West Bromwich, Ajax and Fulham gave before the 1951 Amateur Cup Final.

'Whether you are playing well or badly, want the ball all the time. Win or lose, enjoy the game.'

As Pawson points out, that is the very advice first-class amateurs should be giving to their professional brothers—if only they had not taken the wrong turning.

From *The Evening Standard*, 1975

132

33

Schoolboy Honours

Derek Dougan

Before them, a hundred yards down the lane, was the stadium. Danny had imagined a large, gleaming superstructure with towering floodlights and commissionaires at the doors.

It was a ramshackle wooden place, with a corrugated-iron roof and one small door. A coach and several cars were parked outside, squashing the weeds growing around the stadium. There were no floodlights and he wondered if there were any changing-rooms, or if they had to change at the side of the pitch. A man in a dark blue tracksuit was standing inside the entrance, with a pad, checking names.

'This is Danny Stone,' said Johnson.

The man ticked off his name on the pad and said : 'Dressing-room on the right.'

Johnson left him at the dressing-room door. 'I'll find a seat in the stand,' he said. 'Good luck.'

Danny entered the dressing-room, a ten-foot square box, with three narrow benches and nails to hang clothes on. Bare chests, bare buttocks, bare legs con-fronted him. Clean, supple bodies and hair beginning to sprout under tender arms. A pungent smell of lotion, freshly laundered socks and shirts. He took his boots from his carrier-bag and saw a set of blue and white socks, white shorts and a blue shirt neatly piled on the bench close to the door. He was the last. The shirt was Number 8, so it must be his. No one spoke to him. He did not know who they were, if they had come from one school or ten schools, if they had played together before or just met.

Studs made small dents in the wooden floor as feet were stamped into boots and then laced. Socks were pulled over thick wads of newspaper, making legs look enormous. Danny had no shin-pads. He felt lighter without any.

He changed into the kit and sat waiting for someone to give instructions. He had expected to be greeted and introduced to the officials. The boys were laughing and joking, wrapping laces around their boots in so many layers that Danny thought of the

"Did you see what their right back did to me ...!"

Egyptian mummy he had seen on a school visit to a museum. His own laces were wound once underfoot and once round the heels.

The man who had been at the door came in, blew a whistle and said: 'Right, everyone ready? Let's give 'em a pasting, shall we?'

With a clump of boots, everyone filed out. Danny joined the end of the line, diminutive behind the six-foot, green-jerseyed goalkeeper.

The other side were kicking about in the goal area. A cheer, mingled with handclaps, greeted the county team. Fifty or sixty people were sprinkled around the grandstand. Johnson was by himself in the front row. He waved. Danny scanned the rows to see if Jake Morris was there. He wasn't.

Both goal areas were soggy after overnight rain and a blustery wind was going to make ball control difficult. Conditions were not as Danny liked them. His delicate touch needed calm weather, no more than a breeze, and if he got bogged down in mud he would be useless.

He could avoid the mud by keeping out of the penalty area, which would mean long-distance shooting.

With the wind at his back in the first half, he was set to justify his selection. But it was six or seven minutes before the ball came his way. The Leicestershire side were determined to hold out against the wind in the first half and take advantage of it in the second. They played possession football and Danny began to despair. Nothing was coming his way. His outside-right had fallen back to help in defence. He had most of the right side of the pitch to himself and knew if he got a good pass he would have acres of room in which to move. He tried clapping his hands to draw attention to his advantage. He could have shouted, but he was a new boy and had to wait for them to make use of him.

When he got his first touch of

the ball it was not a pass from one of his own players. The opposing centre-half skidded in the mud as he tried to take a hefty kick down field and sliced the ball to Danny's unmarked position. Nodding it down, Danny had it in his stride and was streaking towards goal, keeping to the dry parts of the pitch, while the Leicestershire defence rushed to block his path. Two yards from the edge of the penalty area he placed a ground shot wide of the advancing goalkeeper and watched the ball skid through the mud into the net. It was a beautiful sight, the ball obeying the instruction of his right foot, flicking particles of mud as it cut a direct line into the far corner of the goal.

Hands were slapping him on the back. 'Bloody good shot, kid.' 'Great goal . . .'

Now the ball came his way. Passes were directed to him. He had shown what he could do and they wanted him to do it again. He didn't disappoint them. He scored two more goals in the first half, one a dipping shot over the goalkeeper's head from fifteen yards and the other a header from a corner.

Against the wind in the second half, he was less conspicuous, but the game had been won, three-nil.

Johnson shook his hand as he came off the pitch.

'Well done, lad, well done.'

In the dressing-room the man in the tracksuit—Danny still didn't know who he was—said to him: 'That's what I call a debut. You know what you get for a hat-trick?'

'Get?'

'This,' he said, handing him the match-ball, wet after it had been washed under a tap.

At first Danny thought he was joking.

'It's yours,' said Tracksuit.

'Mine?'

'Don't you want it?'

'Yes, yes.'

It was the first football he had owned. In his hands it felt huge, majestic, comforting. Clutched to his chest, it felt like a cat or dog that had curled itself into a ball and was allowing him to fondle it, belonging to him.

'Look what they gave me,' he said, when he had changed and was with his headmaster in the corridor, filled now with officials and boys with their parents.

'You deserve it,' said Johnson.

Danny looked around, waiting for the talent scouts to come to him. Where are they? His headmaster couldn't refuse to sign a registration form now. He had represented his county, won the match practically single-handed. The match ball was his. There was bound to be a rush to sign him. That's why they had come, wasn't it, to search for talent, to snatch up future apprentices? What were they waiting for?

'I'd better get you home so you can tell your parents all about it,' said Johnson.

He led the way to the car. Danny delayed, walking slowly, waiting for a hand on his shoulder and a voice saying: 'Just a minute lad. I'd like a word with you.'

At the car door he turned. The stadium door, closed behind him, did not open. No one came. On the journey back he sat with the ball on his knee, caressing it, and then nodding it gently with his forehead. Pinky Blurton, he assured himself, would never snatch this ball away from him—not without a fight. Because he was stronger now and somehow taller.

From *The Footballer*, 1974

"Don't be bleedin' stupid, Ronnie. I can't see how playing for West Ham would intefere wiv anybody's religion."

34

A Bit of a Struggle

Ian Bain

Denis Hunt spent a good part of this summer sowing grass seeds on the pitch at Ashford Town Football Club. He nursed the young grass, cut it when it had grown and put down new turf where it was needed. He pulled out the weeds, painted the goal-posts and gave the stand a brush-up. Then he got down to training his team.

Hunt, 36-year-old former Gillingham full-back, is manager of Southern League Ashford. And if his skills with a hoe and motor mower are less vital than his ability to coach, they were desperately necessary when one more bill might have broken the club's back.

'We just could not afford to bring in contractors,' he says. 'But it had to be done, so we all mucked in—the directors, myself, the youth squad and other volunteers—and we did it ourselves.'

Such teamwork is typical of the survival instinct in Southern League football. Small crowds and big overdrafts have created a spirit of defiance among the Football League cast-offs and aspiring youngsters who go to make up the ranks of the part-time professionals. But it is a spirit not cheaply attained.

For League rejects, coming to terms with second-class soccer is often painful and always harsh. The mutter of applause from 300 spectators when a goal is scored is no substitute for the roar of 20,000 nor the occasional local paper headline an acceptable replacement for *Match of the Day* accolades.

It is only when the glamour of the big-time and the adulation of the fans becomes a memory that they can begin to enjoy, and take a pride in, their new way of life.

Hunt calls this the period of adjustment. 'Many players come to Southern League football feeling that their last manager was wrong in letting them go. They have a chip on their shoulder; they think they should still be with their old club and that they are above non-League football.

'They have to find a job. Some of them, if they've left school at 15 and gone straight into a big club, may arrive in the Southern League at the age of 19 when they've finished their apprenticeship and been told they're not good enough. They've never been to work before and suddenly they have to get up in the morning and travel to some shop or office or go out labouring for eight or nine hours a day.

'For the married man, the transition is particularly difficult. He comes home tired and the wife says, "You're not going out again,' but he has to go and train or play in a mid-week match.'

To the older players, many of whom have edged their way down the divisions, Southern League is a natural progression towards retirement from football.

Tony Bentley, Ashford Town's right back, is 34 and capable of a good few years yet. 'Here's a gem,' he says, 'I'm earning more money now than I was in the first team at Stoke when I was 19. £13 then and about £20 now.'

If inflation makes the comparison meaningless, it is still indicative of the pride that he and other experienced players have in their game. Bentley lives and trains in Southend. He travels 73 miles to each home game and immeasurably more to many of the away ones. Others are equally distant.

Left back Bobby Nash, 28, ex-Queens Park Rangers and now a teacher, lives in Hastings; Trevor Pearce, 25, a one-time Arsenal reserve is a carpenter in Aldershot; several are based in the London area and one in Woking. Some, noticeably, have continued to live near their last League club.

'The problem,' says Bentley, 'is that we don't get the chance to practise the things we do wrong in a match. We don't meet again until the next match and in the meantime all we can do is think about it.'

Trevor Pearce wouldn't mind getting back into League football, but he says, he couldn't afford to. 'I'm not a First or Second Division player and the money the others are paying is not good enough. With my job and the money from Ashford I'm on about £60 a week. In full-time soccer I'd only get about £40.

If the senior players are the backbone of Ashford Town, then the youngsters are the key to the club's economic survival—not through their ability to play the club out of trouble, but purely through their potential in the transfer market. Ashford Town are stoney broke and manager Hunt needs to sell one good young player a year to keep the overdraft within reasonable limits.

'We are likely' he says, 'to lose about £4,000 this season and the same the next. You only have to look at our first couple of games this season to see how deeply in trouble we are. It cost us nearly £400 in travel expenses and wages to play away at Bideford. At our first home game the total receipts with gate money and jackpot tickets came to about

£70. The only way to get those kind of losses back is for me to find a youngster, polish him up and sell him.'

The lack of local support that makes such trading necessary saddens Hunt, who, like his players is a part-timer. With the money he earned from coaching schools while he was at Gillingham he has set up in business as a newsagent.

With a population of about 28,000, Ashford is a fairly pleasant, ordinary market town on the edge of the Downs, less pleasant only when the wind from the east carries the sickly sweet stench of the perfume factory on the small industrial estate. But fewer than 400 of that population turn out each week to watch the team, despite their reasonably attractive style of football and their middle-of-the-table position in Division I South last season.

'People should support their local team,' says Hunt. 'I think it is important for a town to have a senior soccer club. When we travel to Minehead or Dorchester, for instance, we carry the name of the town and people think of Ashford when they wouldn't do otherwise.'

He blames the missing spectators on apathy, the poor state of the ground at Ashford and the over-exposure of football on television.

'The new kind of spectator coming along, the more discriminating youngster, wants better facilities these days, better seating, better toilets, and so on, and

a real professional football atmosphere. He comes into grounds like ours and he feels, well . . . nothing. He goes down the road to Folkestone, say, where there's a brand new stand that's clean and there are no weeds on the pitch and he can sense he's in the right sort of place. But the difference is that Folkestone's ground is maintained by the council which can afford to spend money on it. We can't.'

Ashford are, however, in the process of selling their ground for housing development and are moving into the new sports centre. And if punitive taxation doesn't eat up too much of the profits, Hunt's days of grass planting should be over.

Television, on the other hand, is a cross that they and all the other small clubs will always have to bear. 'People can sit at home and watch your Liverpools, your Arsenals, your Keegans and players like that and when they come down to watch old Harry Brown trip over the bloody ball, they can't understand it. They've got used to a certain standard of game from watching two or three matches on the box every Saturday and Sunday and another in the week and anything less than that they think is rubbish.

'When I was a kid I used to read about Matthews and Finney who were miles away and they were legends. When they came to Portsmouth with Preston or Stoke or Blackpool or whichever club they were with, the crowds used to flock to see them. But now they can see the big stars on the box every week.

'I'm sure that if Sinatra was on television every week, people would get fed up after six weeks. But he makes two appearances a year and you can't get a ticket. You can over-expose anything. You can have too much sex, too much steak, too much beer . . . it must apply to soccer.

'A few years ago it was different. There would be 3,000 at Ashford every week. When I played here with Gillingham in the Cup there was 6,000. Now there are 300.

'I feel really sorry for the people who work damned hard to keep the game alive in Ashford. People like Gladys and Des Hover who run the supporters' club. You can go into their kitchen and find it piled high with jackpot tickets and account books. They work hours and hours and drive all over the place without pay just to keep football going. They are the ones who are being let down by the inhabitants of Ashford.'

Hunt has no great ambitions for the club, save a good run in the FA Cup. 'I could buy one more player, maybe two, and we would stand as good a chance as any of promotion to the Premier Division. But what would promotion bring me? Personal pride,

a night's celebrations at the end of the season and a year of agony, for we are just not equipped financially to compete with the Yeovils and Ketterings.'

But the Cup is different. Every small club manager dreams of leading another Hereford to the glories of Newcastle and West Ham, or better still, bringing a Leeds or Liverpool to their own humble turf. Hunt is no exception.

Ashford began the long road to the vision of Wembley a few weeks ago when they themselves were the giants in the first qualifying round and Deal the would-be killers. After an anxious first half, they outclassed the Kent League side, put four goals in the net and wiped the worry from the brow of Hunt. 'There are going to be some upsets in this season's Cup and I didn't want Ashford to be the first,' he said later.

Skipper Terry Street is certain that his team has the determination to make an impact, however small. 'We are professionals. We are paid to play. But most of us would play for nothing because we simply enjoy it'.

Some would say that the apathetic people of Ashford did not deserve Ashford Town.

From *Sportsworld*, 1974

35

The Game

Dannie Abse

Follow the crowds to where the
   turnstiles click.
The terraces fill. *Hoompa*, blares
   the brassy band.
Saturday afternoon has come to
   Ninian Park
and, beyond the goalposts, in the
   Canon Stand
between black spaces, a hundred
   matches spark.

Waiting, we recall records, legendary scores:
Fred Keenor, Hardy, in a royal blue
   shirt.
The very names, sad as the old
   songs, open doors
before our time where someone
   else was hurt.
Now, like an injured beast, the
   great crowd roars.

The coin is spun. Here all is
   simplified
and we are partisan who cheer the
   Good,
hiss at passing Evil. Was Lucifer
   offside?
A wing falls down when cherubs
   howl for blood.
Demons have agents: the Referee is bribed.

The white ball smacks the crossbar. Satan rose
higher than the others in the
   smoked brown gloom
to sink on grass in a ballet
   dancer's pose.
Again, it seems, we hear a familiar tune
not quite identifiable. A distant
   whistle blows.

Memory of faded games, the
   discarded years;
talk of Aston Villa, Orient, and the
   Swans.
Half-time, the band played the
   same military airs
as when the Bluebirds once were
   champions.
Round touchlines, the same
   cripples in their chairs.

Mephistopheles had his joke. The
   honest team
dribbles ineffectually, no one can
   be blamed.
Infernal backs tackle, inside forwards scheme,
and if they fould us need we be
   ashamed?
Heads up! Oh for a Ted Drake, a
   Dixie Dean.

'Saved!' or else, discontents, we
are transferred
long decades back, like Faust
must pay that fee.
The Night is early. Great phan-
toms in us stir
as coloured jerseys hover, move
diagonally
on the damp turf, and our eidetic
visions blur.

God sign our souls! Because the
obscure Staff
of Hells rules this world, jugular
fans guessed
the result halfway through the
second half

and those who knew the score
just seem depressed.
Small boys swarm the field for an
autograph.

Silent the Stadium. The crowds
have all filed out.
Only the pigeons beneath the
roofs remain.
The clean programmes are
trampled underfoot,
and natural the dark, appropriate
the rain,
whilst, under lampposts, threatening newsboys shout.

ANDY CAPP

OH, DEAR! THAT LOOKS AWFUL, PET! WHAT'VE THEY DONE T' YER?!

OWW! ME KNEE~!

IT'S OKAY, FLO, I THINK I CAN WALK ALL RIGHT

2252

I'LL SAY THIS F'YER, KID — YOU'VE GOT GUTS

ACTUALLY, IT'S ONLY A SLIGHT GRAZE, BUT IF I DON'T MAKE A FUSS, 'E DOES — AN' IT TAKES 'IM LONGER!

142

Acknowledgements

Acknowledgements and thanks are due to the following authors, publishers, newspapers and television companies:

To John Moynihan and Quartet Books Ltd. for two extracts from *Football Fever*.

To Ian Campbell and BBC TV for 'We Are The Champions'.

To Alan Ross for 'Football Grounds of the Riviera' and 'Stanley Matthews'.

To Alan Simpson and Hampton Town Football Club for 'A Voice In The Crowd'.

To Brian Glanville and Martin Secker & Warburg Ltd. for 'Greenberg' from *The Thing He Loves and Other Stories*.

To Hunter Davies and Weidenfeld & Nicholson Ltd. for 'European Football' from *The Glory Game*.

To Tony Pawson and *The Guardian* for 'Days of Pegasus Past at Wembley'.

To *Sportsworld* for 'Away From It All' by Willis Hall.

To John Bird and John Wells and Yorkshire Television for 'Television Coverage' from *Leeds Athletic*.

To Mike Langley and the *People* for 'Bill Shankly'.

To Jane Gaskell and the *Daily Mail* for '. . . And His Wife'.

To The Argentine Football Association for 'As She Is Spoken'.

To A.J. Ayer and the Statesmen & Nation Publishing Co. Ltd. for 'Double Top'.

To Ian Davies and *Sportsworld* for 'Kicking The Habit'.

To Hutchinson & Co. Ltd., the FA, and Richard Bates for 'The Manchester United Disaster' by H.E. Bates.

To Peter Terson and Penguin Books Ltd. for 'Religious Fervour' from *Zigger-Zagger*.

To Julie Welch and *The Observer* for 'Burnley v. Newcastle United' and 'West Ham v. Manchester United'.

To Ian Wooldridge and the *Daily Mail* for 'The Very Last Word' and 'The Groundsman'.

To Dannie Abse and Hutchinson & Co. Ltd., for 'The Game'.

To John Arlott and *The Guardian* for 'Christmas With Regnar'.

To Hugh McIlvanney and Sportsworld for 'Many Happier Returns'.

To Hutchinson & Co. Ltd., for 'All Mod Cons' from *George Best* by Michael Parkinson.

To Jack Rosenthal and Granada Television for 'Single-Minded' from *The Dustbinmen*.

To Michael Carey and *The Guardian* for 'Annual General Pantomime'.

To Peter Cole and *The Guardian* for 'Frankfurt, June 1974'.

To Arthur Hopcraft and Collins Publishers for 'The Referee' from *The Football Man*.

To Bernard Joy and the *Evening Standard* for 'Goodbye to All That'.

To Derek Dougan and Allison & Busby Ltd. for 'Schoolboy Honours' from *The Footballer*.

To Ian Bain and *Sportsworld* for 'A Bit of A Struggle'.

143

To Geoffrey Green and *The Times* for 'Leeds United v. Ujpest Dozsa', and 'England v. Portugal'.
To the artist and *Foul* and *Punch* for the Bill Tidy cartoons.
To Reg Smythe and the *Daily Mirror* for the Andy Capp cartoons.
The Focus on Fact Soccer Strip by Gary Keane and Neville Randall is reproduced by permission of the *Daily Mail*, London.

"Last week he was checking on hotels for the England team.   This week it's the pubs."